IMAGES
of America

SALT LAKE CITY'S
HISTORIC ARCHITECTURE

This aerial view from around 1915 of the intersection of South Temple and State Streets shows important Salt Lake City buildings built over half a century. At the bottom left are Brigham Young's Lion and Beehive Houses, erected in the mid-1850s. To the right is the Gardo House, built in the 1870s. On the southeast corner are the Alta Club of 1897–1898 and the Salt Lake City Library of 1905, both extant. Just left of the trolley car are the Eagle Gate Apartments, since replaced by a less elegant replica. Farther up South Temple Street, the towers of the Cathedral of the Madeleine dominate the city's "Street of Mansions."

ON THE COVER: The monumental City and County Building was built from 1891 to 1894. Local architect Henry Monheim teamed with Bird and Proudfoot of Des Moines to design the Romanesque Revival landmark. Restored and made earthquake-resistant in the 1980s, the civic edifice served as the first state capitol until the present capitol was completed in 1915.

IMAGES
of America

SALT LAKE CITY'S
HISTORIC ARCHITECTURE

Allen Dale Roberts

ARCADIA
PUBLISHING

Published by Arcadia Publishing
Charleston, South Carolina

Printed in the United States of America

Library of Congress Control Number: 2012941181

For all general information, please contact Arcadia Publishing:
Telephone 843-853-2070
Fax 843-853-0044
E-mail sales@arcadiapublishing.com
For customer service and orders:
Toll-Free 1-888-313-2665

Visit us on the Internet at www.arcadiapublishing.com

To Salt Lake City's gone and often forgotten owners,
architects, and builders, who gave us the rich legacy
of historic architecture we enjoy today

CONTENTS

ACKNOWLEDGMENTS

I express my deep appreciation to those who have helped make this book possible, including Doug Misner and Heidi Orchard of the Utah State Historical Society Library, historical consultant Randall Dixon, photograph editor Elisabeth Carroll, graphic designer Robert Holman, and acquisitions editor Stacia Bannerman and production editor Tim Sumerel of Arcadia Publishing. The vast majority of images in this book are historical photographs used by permission of the Utah State Historical Society. The relatively few recent photographs were taken by the author.

Mining magnate Samuel Newhouse was the catalyst for creating what is now called the Exchange Place Historic District. Among its extant landmarks are the Commercial Club (1907–1908), at the lower left; Stock Exchange (1908), at the bottom right; Boston and Newhouse Buildings, (1908–1911) beyond; and Post Office/Federal Building (1903, plus additions), at the western terminus of Exchange Place. Intended to be the "Wall Street of the West," this commercial district was built to provide a competitive alternative to the Mormon-dominated business center three blocks to the north. Two matching towers and a theater were to have been built at the east end of the street, but Newhouse's later financial reversals precluded their construction.

INTRODUCTION

Salt Lake City enjoys a rich architectural heritage. Residents' appreciation of and desire for good design had its genesis in Kirtland, Ohio, and Nauvoo, Illinois, cities of substantial—even monumental—buildings created by the Mormons more than a decade before they first entered the Great Salt Lake Valley in 1847. They brought with them builder-architects, skilled craftsmen, tools, architectural guidebooks, city plans, and their previous design and construction experience. With this background and fueled by religious zeal, they methodically began to survey and lay out a city, harvest lumber, start an adobe yard, and construct the full range of buildings needed to support a burgeoning population. In their minds, they were making the desert blossom like a rose, a metaphor for building their Zion homeland.

Joseph Smith, Brigham Young, and other key church founders were well informed about architecture and interested in creating buildings of style, which would reflect well on their culture. Young eschewed log and wood-frame buildings in favor of permanent masonry structures, initially of adobe on stone foundations. Within a decade, the city had a social hall, a tabernacle, a city hall, a council hall, church meetinghouses, schools, stores, mills, and houses—mostly in the Greek Revival style, with some in the Early Gothic Revival style. Due to a paucity of coal and wood fuel, fired brick was not available here until 1863, when it began to replace adobe as the preferred masonry.

Architecture is limited by creativity but also by technology and the building materials available. All of these factors were quickly advanced by the arrival of the railroad in 1869, which brought talented, widely experienced architects and builders from Europe and the eastern states, as well as a flood of diverse building materials not previously available. It also allowed for easier traveling and greater access to the rainbow of ideas in the outside world. As the city's isolation decreased in the 1870s, a flourishing of architectural expression occurred. Three- and four-story buildings of brick and iron replaced the initial one- and two-story adobe structures. New styles appeared, starting with the French Second Empire and Victorian Italianate in the 1870s and 1880s and the picturesque family of Victorian styles from the late 1880s through the 1890s and beyond. These included the Queen Anne, Victorian Romanesque, Victorian Eclectic, Shingle, and Eastlake styles. During the same decades, a countervailing classical movement was in vogue, bringing Neoclassical Revival, Beaux-Arts, Chateauesque, and Georgian Revival expressions.

Commercial, industrial, governmental, social, educational, and religious architecture also made great advances as technology, materials, and styles evolved. The advent of steel-frame and reinforced concrete construction led to the city's first "skyscrapers," beginning around 1900. Brought in by immigrant architects attracted by the city's building booms or imitated by local architects made aware of stylistic trends through professional magazines, new American styles like Romanesque Revival, Richardsonian Romanesque, Second Renaissance Revival, and Commercial Style appeared downtown. While it is true that most architecture—like most art, music, and literature—is largely derivative, individual creativity resulted in impressive local variations. The introduction of new materials like terra-cotta, cast concrete, aluminum, and plate glass also changed the face of early-20th-century buildings.

After 1900, new American styles evolved and flourished locally, among them the Bungalow, Arts and Crafts, Prairie, and Art Deco styles. Especially after World War I, several revival styles also made an appearance, including American and Spanish Colonial, and Egyptian, Byzantine, English Tudor, Elizabethan, Jacobean, Mission, and Norman revivals.

Historic preservation has played a vital role in restoring Salt Lake City's architectural heritage. Of the 220 buildings described herein, 60 have been destroyed, including a surprising number of highly significant landmarks. Yet 160 remain and of these, 124 have been substantially restored, renovated, or continuously maintained. Twenty are extant but have not been renovated. Another three have had their facades hidden behind newer ones. The buildings in these last two categories are good candidates for future restoration.

I am personally familiar with many of these buildings, either through preservation efforts or because my architectural firm, Cooper Roberts Simonsen Associates (CRSA), has designed their restoration or renovation. CRSA has been involved with 45 of these historic building preservation projects, which underscores my interest in the subject.

These important structures built along South Temple (formerly Brigham Street) by the Church of Jesus Christ of Latter-day Saints are still extant today. From right to left, they are the Eagle Gate (1859/1963), Beehive House (1852–1854), Lion House (1854–1856), Church Administration Building (1917) and Hotel Utah (1909–1911), now called the Joseph Smith Memorial Building. In the late 20th century, each of these historically and architecturally significant buildings was restored, and they remain in beneficial use.

One
CIVIC AND PUBLIC ARCHITECTURE

The design for the Salt Lake City and County Building, built from 1891 to 1894, was the result of an architectural competition won by the team of Monheim, Bird, and Proudfoot. German-born Henry Monheim was elected the first president of the Salt Lake City Institute of Architects in 1891, and Bird and Proudfoot was a Des Moines–based firm. The largest and most flamboyant example of the Romanesque Revival style in Utah, the City and County Building served as the state capitol between Utah statehood in 1896 and 1915, when the present capitol was completed. A major restoration effort in the 1980s provided a seismic-resistant design with the installation of an innovative base isolation system of rubber and steel cylinders under the original foundation.

The council hall was the first of three major civic structures of similar appearance built in the pre-1869 pioneer era. Before its destruction by fire in 1883, it sat just south of Temple Square. Built in 1849–1850, the 45-foot-square structure featured stone walls, a hip roof, and a cupola. It was designed by Truman O. Angell to house meetings of the General Assembly of the Provisional State of Deseret—precursor to the state of Utah. It was also an early home to the LDS Salt Lake Stake High Council, the first presidency of the LDS Church, the first Utah Territorial Library, the *Deseret News,* and the University of Deseret (later the University of Utah).

Some local buildings are so revered that replicas were made after they were demolished, while others were moved or reconstructed, as occurred in 1962–1963 with the two-story, red sandstone city hall. Designed by architect William H. Folsom and built from 1863 to 1866, the 60-foot-square, Federal/Greek Revival–style building was both city hall and territorial capitol until 1894. When deemed obsolete, it was dismantled and rebuilt south of the new capitol. Its octagonal cupola, balustrades, brackets, and stone pilasters and lintels are distinctive.

After Utah achieved statehood in 1896, the federal presence in the city intensified and this was the city's first major federal building. Clad with stone, the exterior was Beaux-Arts classicism in style. The seven-bay-wide facade features engaged and fluted Corinthian columns, an ornate, classical balustrade, and horizontal, smooth-cut stone banding.

The oldest building in the Exchange Place Historic District is the joint post office and federal courts building constructed in two sections, starting with the northern section built between 1903 and 1906. It was designed by James K. Taylor, the supervising architect for the federal Department of the Treasury. He was assisted by local architect Walter J. Cooper, who was working in Salt Lake City for New York architect Henry Ives Cobb, the designer of the Boston and Newhouse Buildings. The long east facade is Neoclassical Revival in style, as evidenced by its 15 engaged, fluted columns, and its classical entablature and balustrade. The matching southern section was added around 1930. Now the Moss Federal Courthouse, it is being renovated as part of a block-sized project, which includes the construction of a large, modern courthouse.

According to former architect of the capitol David Hart, the Utah State Capitol was named in a recent survey as one of the three most beautiful state capitols in the United States. After undergoing a recent $200 million restoration, which removed intrusive interior additions, provided base isolation seismic-resistant design, and returned it to its original historic appearance, the accolade is well deserved. Local classicist architect Richard K.A. Kletting won a national design competition and provided a Neoclassical Revival design inspired by the national capitol and earlier state capitols. Designed in 1912, the 404-foot-long, granite-clad, reinforced concrete structure was completed in 1915. Its massive, copper-roofed dome encloses a 165-foot-tall rotunda.

The capitol's elegant interior features polished classical columns of Georgia marble supporting the walkways surrounding the spacious, open atrium. The interior is illuminated by two long skylights flanking the rotunda and flooding the entire three-story interior space with natural light. The recent restoration removed non-original walls and returned the building to its 1912 floor plan. The great central rotunda remains a favorite location for receptions, public gatherings, and speeches. Its significant interiors include the house, senate, and supreme court chambers and the visually rich Gold Room.

The former Salt Lake City Library is considered Utah's best example of the classically ornate Beaux-Arts style, which flourished in America from about 1890 to 1920. Named after the École des Beaux-Arts, the famous school of arts and architecture in Paris, the style received great impetus from the 1893 World's Fair in Chicago. Local architect Frederick A. Hale teamed with the prestigious New York firm of Hines and LaFarge to design this delightful, three-story, limestone-clad house for books, built in 1905. Decades later, it housed the Hansen Planetarium. In recent years, the exterior was meticulously restored, but the interior was mostly removed to accommodate its new occupant, O.C. Tanner Jewelry.

Built at the head of Main Street, the Pioneer Memorial Museum was erected in 1949–1950 by the Daughters of the Utah Pioneers and the State of Utah. Its exterior is an approximate, terra-cotta-clad replica of the beloved Salt Lake Theatre, razed in 1928. The museum exhibits thousands of pioneer artifacts, among them the original wooden eagle that loomed over State Street's Eagle Gate, designed by Culers and Young.

A west side landmark, the Chapman Branch Library was designed by Joseph Don Carlos Young, a son of LDS Church president and Utah governor Brigham Young, and built in 1918. The classically columned entry faces an intersection at a 45-degree angle, and its small interior nevertheless housed an ambitious 30,000-volume collection. It was one of six Salt Lake City libraries funded by the Carnegie Corporation. Following a major fire, it was renovated in 1994 and converted to a community center.

The Sprague Library serves the city's Sugarhouse neighborhood. Opened in 1928, its exterior is Jacobean Revival in style, featuring a steeply pitched, slate-shingled roof and light-colored quoins, parapets, and door and window trim. Named for Joanna Sprague, the head librarian for the Salt Lake City Public Library system for 37 years, it was renovated in 1990 and expanded in 2001 and continues in its original use. The building was designed by Ashton and Evans.

Two
RELIGIOUS
ARCHITECTURE

Soon after their arrival in the Salt Lake Valley, the pioneers laid out a city plan of 660-foot-square blocks separated by 108-foot-wide streets on a strict north-south, east-west grid. One of these 10-acre blocks was designated Temple Square, upon which the Mormons started their Great Temple (right) in 1853. Before it was completed 40 years later, other buildings, including the Tabernacle (center) and Assembly Hall (left) were finished. Each year, more than four million visitors tour Temple Square.

The first large building constructed on Temple Square was the 64-foot-by-126-foot adobe tabernacle, erected in 1851–1852. It seated 2,500 people. The symmetrical front facade had ornamental wood bargeboards and a carved sun face under emanating light rays in a gable-end triangle. The tabernacle was designed by Truman O. Angell, Brigham Young's architect for all the city's earliest religious and public structures.

To achieve the Salt Lake Tabernacle's clear-spanning—without columns or beams—vaulted interior ceiling, engineer Henry Grow innovatively employed a complex wooden-lattice truss system he had seen used on bridges in eastern states. The trusses were cross-braced, and the connections secured with wooden dowels and leather straps shrunken and tightened with water. Note the forest of scaffolding.

Sometimes called the Great Tabernacle, this world-famous building was constructed between 1863 and 1867 and measures 150 feet by 250 feet, with semicircular ends. It is built with red sandstone piers supporting an elliptical, clear-spanning roof. The interior is known for its excellent acoustics and seats 8,000. This unique structure is the work of four important designers: project architect William H. Folsom, interior architect Truman O. Angell, truss designer and structural engineer Henry Grow, and organ designer Joseph Ridges, who created the elaborate frontispiece for the 1,600-pipe organ. Originally, the round roof was covered with one million machine-sawn cedar shingles. Later, it was sheathed with the present metal roofing.

The Tabernacle's interior is one great, arched, open space. The pews are made of pine, hand-grained to resemble oak; and the balcony was added early on to increase the seating capacity. In the rear is the tiered rostrum area, and behind it is the seating for the famed 300-plus-member Mormon Tabernacle Choir. The ornamental organ frontispiece features large pipes hollowed out from logs hauled to Salt Lake City from Pine Valley, 300 miles to the south. The Tabernacle was recently renovated and seismically upgraded.

Said to be built from granite blocks rejected from the Salt Lake Temple's construction, the 60-foot-by-120-foot Assembly Hall is architecturally significant in its own right. It was designed by Mormon convert and San Francisco architect Obed Taylor, who also designed the similar Coalville Tabernacle, modified from the same plans, as well as the famous Zion's Cooperative Mercantile Institution (ZCMI) cast-iron storefront. The hall's landmark exterior includes pinnacled buttresses and a graceful, 130-foot-tall central tower. The two-story interior features a horseshoe-shaped balcony, exposed organ pipes, and vaulted ceilings.

It took 40 years, from 1853 to 1893, to construct the Salt Lake Temple. The original architect, Truman O. Angell, died in 1887, so the interior design and towers were completed by Brigham Young's son Joseph Don Carlos Young. Built of local granite, the stylistically eclectic temple was described by the architect Young as "Romanesque modified by the Castellated style." The six-spired exterior is rich in carved stone symbolism, including an "alpha and omega" scroll, clasped hands, an all-seeing eye, and the Big Dipper star group. Measuring 118 feet by 186 feet in plan, the Temple's walls are 16, 12, and 8 feet thick, to last through the Second Coming. The east-central tower is the tallest at 210 feet, and atop it is a 12-foot-tall, gilded statue of the trumpeting Angel Moroni, a Book of Mormon figure. The temple's interior is used exclusively by faithful Mormons and is not open to the public.

Assembly Hall architect Obed Taylor designed the Gothic Revival 18th Ward Meetinghouse, which was built from 1881 to 1883. In 1973, it was dismantled and reconstructed anew in 1980 just south of the state capitol grounds. Its steeple tower, buttresses, and pointed windows are typical of the Gothic Revival style. Now known as the White Chapel, it is available for public gatherings and weddings.

"19th Ward House of Worship 1890" reads the carved stone plaque over the front entry of this unusual meetinghouse—the only one built by the LDS Church to have a Byzantine-influenced onion-dome tower and pinnacles. Attributed to architect-builder Robert H. Bowman, the building's unique design may be due to its Victorian Eclectic styling, or perhaps it was a conscious effort to send a message that Mormonism was now a worldwide faith rather than an isolated, Utah-bound religion. Around 1970, the church was sold to the city and converted to a community and performing arts center.

Although not a Mormon himself, eventual state capitol architect Richard K.A. Kletting designed the imposing Granite Stake Tabernacle, dedicated in 1903. Such massive corner towers are rare in Mormon tabernacles. The interior featured a great dome spanning the chapel with groin vaults. Despite its size and impressive architecture, it was replaced only 25 years later by the newer Granite Tabernacle on 900 East (below) and then razed in about 1962.

This Granite Stake Tabernacle replaced the giant 1903 one in 1930 at a cost of $225,000. Edward O. Anderson and Lorenzo Snow Young were its architects, and the style was described at the time as "Spanish Romanesque." The exterior features colorful fieldstone on its first level and a narrow steeple, all trimmed in Spanish motifs of terra-cotta.

The 27th Ward Meetinghouse was built in the Avenues in the English Parish Church Gothic style in 1902. It features numerous art glass, Gothic windows, and an architecturally compatible cultural hall, attached to its south side in 1928 by Ashton and Evans. John E. Robinson was the architect of the original building, and the design was so popular that more than 40 of these chapels were built church-wide.

Only the Gothic art glass window remains from this English Parish Church Gothic–style 17th Ward Mormon Meetinghouse built in 1907. When it was razed in the 1970s, the historic front window was placed in the new, replacement chapel. This popular church design was replicated in other locations. The prototype was created by non-Mormon architects Ware and Treganza, and it bears a strong resemblance to Protestant religious architecture of the period.

Three buildings remain from what was originally a six-building ecclesiastical complex serving the 10th Ward. To the right is the city's best pioneer-era Mormon meetinghouse—a brick, Greek Revival–style edifice, which features a semicircular plaque in the upper gable reading, "Erected 1873, John Proctor, Bishop." The English Parish Gothic–style church at the left was designed by Cannon and Fetzer and built in 1909. It features a large, Gothic-arched art glass window depicting Jesus Christ. Out of sight is Richard Kletting's 1887 school, now used as classrooms.

Built in 1908, the Second Ward Meetinghouse was also built in the English Parish Gothic style. It features a square vestry tower set at an angle to the street, and large, pictorial, art glass windows set in Gothic openings. The Ashton Brothers were its architect-builders.

Built in 1907, the 24th Ward Meetinghouse is unusual in that is was custom-designed to fit on this small, sloping, triangular site. The resulting design by architects Young and Young—Brigham Young's progeny—was a unique floor plan with a rounded apse on its narrower north side and a wider section to the south containing a chapel above and amusement hall below. The exterior is Victorian Romanesque. In the 1980s, it was renovated for the offices of Cooper/Roberts Architects, a firm specializing in historic building restoration design.

Most early-1900s LDS ward meetinghouses featured towers or steeples to give them an ecclesiastical character, but the 31st Ward Meetinghouse is an exception, depending instead on pilasters topped by finials and contrasted with horizontal belt courses. Designed by Joseph Don Carlos Young, the L-shaped, split-level building was built in 1902.

At least five Utah architects worked in the Chicago area while Frank Lloyd Wright was developing his radically new Prairie Style. As a result, there seem to be as many Prairie Style buildings in Utah as there are in any location outside of Illinois, among them at least 50 LDS churches. One of the largest, the hilltop Ensign Ward, was designed by the architects Monson and Price and built from 1913 to 1915, at a cost of $50,000. It was razed in the 1980s.

Designed by Pope and Burton—architects of the Cardston Temple, in Alberta, Canada—the First Ward Meetinghouse was considered a landmark example of pure Prairie Style architecture. It was designed in 1913 and bears a striking resemblance to Frank Lloyd Wright's Larkin Building. Split-level in floor plan, its chapel was beautifully illuminated by clerestory windows. It was razed in the late 1970s to the considerable chagrin of preservationists. Note the Wrightian ornament in cast concrete at the top of the main, front piers.

The broad facade of the Colonial Revival–style Yale Ward Meetinghouse was designed by architects Woolley and Evans and built from 1924 to 1926. Although he had worked for and traveled with Frank Lloyd Wright, Taylor Woolley entirely abandoned all Wrightian influences in this design.

The Highland Park Ward was built in 1925, employing a Tudor Revival style devised by architects Pope and Burton. Its not-quite-symmetrical facade features steeply pitched roofs, half-timbering, and small, diamond-shaped windowpanes like those found in English buildings.

St. Mark's Episcopal Cathedral Church was likely the first building in Utah designed by a nationally renowned architect. The office of Richard Upjohn and his son, the presumed architect Richard Michell Upjohn, designed the edifice. English-born cofounders of the American Institute of Architects in 1856, the famous pair worked together from 1853 to 1872 and led the American Early Gothic Revival movement. St. Marks was built of local red sandstone from 1869 to 1871. Its key feature is its gabled belfry, typical of Upjohn churches in the eastern United States. The steeply pitched roof, buttresses, and front rose window are typically Gothic Revival. Its interior nave features a vaulted ceiling and a Scottish-built 1857 organ.

Built mid-block behind and attached to a larger hospital structure and still visible only from mid-block, the diminutive Holy Cross Chapel is the oldest remaining Roman Catholic building in the city. It is a two-story stone and brick sanctuary designed by Carl M. Neuhausen and erected in 1904 for use by hospital patrons and staff. The Gothic Romanesque–style building has round-arched, art glass windows; buttresses; an octagonal lantern; half-round apse; and an artistically realized chapel interior.

The city's first monumental piece of Jewish architecture was the B'nai Israel Temple, built in 1890 of Kyune sandstone in a refined, monochromatic Romanesque Revival style. The central, octagonal dome and lantern are distinctive, as are the large, Roman-arched, art glass windows. The temple was designed by Philip Meyer, who died in a German concentration camp during World War II, and Henry Monheim, co-architect of the City and County Building. Meyer patterned the building after the Great Synagogue in Berlin. The Salt Lake City structure is now in commercial use..

Salt Lake City's second Jewish synagogue was built in 1903 for the Congregation Montifiore. It was designed by German-born architect Carl M. Neuhausen not long before his death in 1907. His symmetrical, Byzantine-influenced design features twin, onion-domed towers with Moorish arches, a Roman-arched front entry and round gable window, both with six-pointed Stars of David. The building's name is written in Hebrew high in the gable. The brick has been painted multiple colors, giving it a mottled, shimmering look.

The significant and enduring presence of the Catholic Church in Salt Lake City is manifest in its superlative Cathedral of the Madeleine, constructed over a decade, from 1899 to 1909. Its twin towers and rose-windowed front gable loom over South Temple Street. The cathedral was designed by Carl M. Neuhausen in a Gothic-Romanesque style of rusticated and smooth-cut Kyune sandstone. Neuhausen died during its construction, and Bernard O. Mecklenburg finished designing the roof and towers. The cathedral's elegance was recaptured during major restorations in the 1970s and 1990s.

The Cathedral of the Madeleine's interior was enhanced by a $10 million restoration, which brought back the colors, textures, and missing elements of the grand space. From the art glass windows made in Munich to the intricately carved woodwork, ornate plasterwork, frescoes and murals, colorfully painted columns, and ribbed vaults, icons, alters, baptistry, and confessionals, this nave is one of the most awe-inspiring interiors in the city. The cathedral's third architect, John Comes, brought in Felix Lieftucher to design the highly ornate interior elements.

Prolific Salt Lake City architect Frederick A. Hale's massive corner tower design for the First Methodist Church fit its corner site. The Victorian Eclectic exterior features Roman-arched windows under curvilinear parapets, evoking a Spanish Baroque feeling. Built in 1905, the sanctuary is illuminated by large art glass windows. It was renovated in the 1980s.

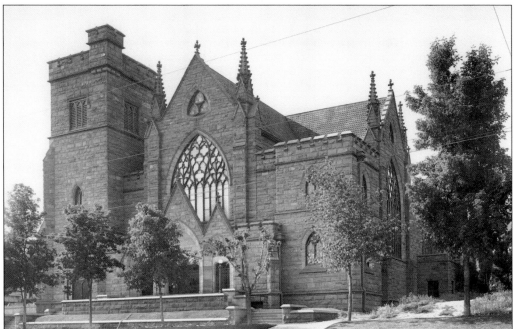

Walter E. Ware, of the leading architectural firm Ware & Treganza, designed the First Presbyterian Church, using Carlisle Cathedral in Scotland as a model. Built in 1905 of local red sandstone, it represents the high point in his design of religious structures. Its style is Medieval Parrish Church Gothic, complete with a square corner tower, buttresses, pinnacles, steeply pitched gables, and a massive Gothic art glass window. The church has been well maintained and experienced a recent, sensitively executed interior restoration.

Built in 1898 and designed by Walter E. Ware, the former First Church of Christ, Scientist has most recently been used as an antiques store. Ware's two-story design is Victorian Romanesque in style, with its rusticated Roman arches trimming the redbrick and sandstone exterior. Foliated, carved capitals and art glass windows add elegance to this relatively small composition.

The large Emmanuel Baptist Church is the city's best use of Neoclassical Revival styling in religious architecture. Its two-story, Ionic-columned south and west porticos dominate the corner site. At two and a half stories, the church is monumental and architecturally intact. It was designed by Swedish-born architect John Headlund and built from 1908 to 1910.

The Byzantine Revival architecture of the Holy Trinity Greek Orthodox Cathedral is unique in the city. Original Byzantine architecture developed from the fourth century to the 15th century and was characterized by large domes, round-arched windows, foliated capitals, and elaborate interior spaces—all features of this cathedral. Key exterior features include the five-columned entry portico, two domed corner towers, a polygonal central tower, and tall art glass windows. The 550-seat interior features a sky-blue domed ceiling, frescoes, murals, and paintings, an altar, icons, carved figures, and shrines. It was built from 1923 to 1925 with Pope and Burton as the local architects and N.A. Dokas of Chicago consulting on the Greek/Byzantine design features. The edifice has been restored and expanded by the vital Greek community.

This neighborhood church was built in 1909 for the United, or Tabor, Danish Evangelical Lutheran congregation. The official architect was Richard K.A. Kletting, but it may have been designed by his intern, Theodore Lauridsen. The church's Late Gothic Revival style is atypical of Kletting's other, more classical works. The thin, elegant steeple tower and its recessed Gothic entry dominate the corner. Attached to the north side is a small rectory.

Prior to being replaced with the present Buddhist temple, this earlier two-story temple served the Buddhist community. Built in 1924, its design is a clear departure from any kind of Christian architecture. The flat facade has a commercial character, but the roof and window treatment and especially the ornamental trim suggest Asian influences. The swastikas were put over the doorways well before the Nazis appropriated the motif; they symbolize well-being and benediction.

Built from 1924 to 1928, this small, Tudor/Gothic Revival–style church was constructed across the street from the Buddhist temple, creating a small grotto of Asian religious edifices. A few Japanese and Chinese immigrants chose to stay in the city after completing their work on the railroads. In 1890, there were 467 Japanese residents in the state, and by 1920, there were 3,000. A group who became Christians erected this one-story church sponsored by the Presbyterians. Its lovely Gothic window with cast-stone tracery and a Tudor-arched entry are both Christian features.

Built in 1901, St. Paul's Episcopal Church is a brightly colored stone and half-timbered building designed by Pope and Burton, with consulting design by an architect named Hill, in the Elizabethan/ Gothic Revival style. Its multicolored stone walls, gabled steeple tower, half-timbering, and English Gothic–style windows are typical of the architecture. To the left is a compatibly designed, half-timbered 1990s addition.

With its broad, columned portico and central steeple tower, the Colonial-style First Unitarian Church would be at home in any New England town. It was designed by local architect Slack Winburn, teamed with the Boston firm of Smith and Walker. Built in 1927 and expanded to the south to include Elliot Hall in 1960, the edifice is now being expanded again to the north. Consistent with its exterior style, this church's interior has a Colonial character, with curving stairways and balcony; a left-side pulpit; tall, Roman-arched windows; and classical cornices.

Three

COMMERCIAL AND OFFICE ARCHITECTURE

This Main Street view from the 1870s shows one of the city's most important pioneer commercial buildings, the Eagle Emporium (right). With its classical facade of red sandstone, it clearly dominated its neighboring smaller adobe and frame structures. Built of brick and stone in 1863–1864, its architect was English-born Utah immigrant William Paul, who also designed the magnificent Devereaux House (page 110). It was built to house William Jenning's dry goods store and banking enterprise. Utah's first millionaire, Jennings also served a term as mayor and in the Utah Territorial Legislature. When the Mormon Church established the Zion's Cooperative Mercantile Institution (ZCMI) network in 1868, Jennings, one of its organizers, leased his emporium to ZCMI as its first store.

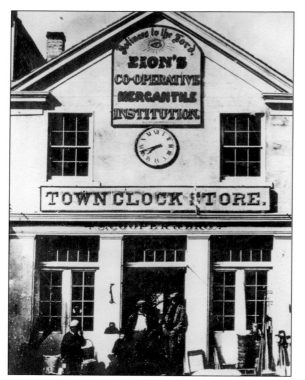

The Town Clock Store was one of many Mormon commercial establishments in the ZCMI system. The store was built in the Greek Revival style in 1860 by architect-builder Charles H. King. The faithful were told to patronize the ZCMIs in an attempt to keep them viable while in competition with Gentile merchants. Note the sign with an all-seeing eye under "Holiness to the Lord," perhaps intended to promote honest business dealings.

Beneath the 1916, Neoclassical Revival, terra-cotta exterior of this diminutive two-story bank is the oldest commercial building in the city—the former Eagle Emporium. Since 1890, Zion's First National Bank has occupied the building. This existing Neoclassical facade was designed by Don Carlos Young, Brigham Young's grandson. The exterior was restored in 2009–2010. Note the freestanding clock and post, installed in 1873 and originally water-powered.

The four Walker brothers, from Canada, became very successful businessmen through their banking and mercantile endeavors. Their classically designed, stone-clad bank was one of the most impressive business buildings during the pioneer era. Built in the 1860s and designed by English-born-and-trained architect E.L.T. Harrison, it stood until the 1920s—decades longer than its adobe neighbors.

A small but impressive 1866 commercial structure was the Wells Fargo & Co. Express, with its classical-style stone facade. All of its windows were round-arched, and the pilasters, carved stone lintels, brackets, and dentils were well executed. It was designed by William H. Folsom and originally housed the Holladay Overland Mail & Express.

This gem of a pioneer commercial facade is so valued that it has been moved twice. The red sandstone storefront now resides in the LDS Church's new City Creek Center project. It is the only commercial facade to survive from the pre-1870 pioneer era. Built in 1869 as Amussen's Jewelry, owned by Carl Christian Amussen, it was proclaimed to be the first fireproof building in the Utah Territory. This was because of its stone superstructure, slate roof, plastered interior walls, and the placement of inert ash between the floor joists. Its architect was William H. Folsom, better known for his designs of the Salt Lake Theatre, the Tabernacle, Salt Lake City Hall, and the Manti Temple.

In this unassuming First National Bank commercial facade is one of the most architecturally significant storefronts in Utah. Its importance is related to its architect—Richard Michell Upjohn of New York—and to it being the oldest cast-iron storefront in Utah, built in 1871. Upjohn was the son and business partner of the leading American Gothic Revival architect, Richard M. Upjohn of England. Upjohn was already in the city working on St. Mark's Episcopal Cathedral (1869–1871). These two projects were the first in Utah designed by a nationally prominent architect. The bank was built for Warren Hussey, and the building later housed the Masonic Lodge and Library, Wells Fargo, and the offices of Simon Bamberger, a German Jew elected governor of Utah in 1916. The First National Bank may be most important unrestored historic building in downtown Salt Lake City.

When built in 1876, the ZCMI building stood proud and alone on Main Street. Its pride came from its new, classically designed cast-iron facade. The storefront was designed by former San Francisco architect and new Salt Lake City resident Obed Taylor. He also designed the south extension (below) in 1880, after which the slightly wider north addition was copied in 1901, designed by Samuel T. Whitaker. This Italianate-influenced cast-iron storefront was the largest ever built in Utah.

The present ZCMI facade has twice been dismantled, restored, and returned to its original Main Street location. It is shown here prior to any preservation efforts. State-of-the-art when built, ZCMI is said to have been America's first documented department store. It was the flagship of a system that operated hundreds of smaller co-op stores throughout the 600-town Mormon Corridor.

This front elevation drawing shows the architect's conception of how the Daft Building would look. It includes a little sign across the central second-floor windows reading: "Harrison & Nichols Architects." The narrow Daft Block is the most intact and visually impressive Queen Anne–style building in the city's commercial district. Its angular bay window and highly ornamental, polychromatic facade are characteristically Victorian. The block is one of the few commercial buildings constructed for a female entrepreneur, Sarah Daft. She later built the Daft Home, for homeless women (see page 78). Daynes Jewelry took over the building in 1908 and occupied it for many decades.

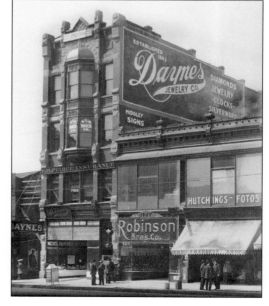

Built from 1887 to 1889, the Daft Block is the work of Elias L.T. Harrison, an English Mormon convert who had studied architecture in London. He arrived here in 1861, became the first to teach classes in architecture, and also designed the new Salt Lake Theatre's highly ornate interior. Over the next 40 years, he designed several important buildings, including William S. Godbe's exuberant Gothic Revival house (page 109). Harrison helped produce the region's first magazine, *Peep O'Day*, the forerunner to the *Salt Lake Tribune*. He was also the spokesman for the reformist, Godbeite New Movement of the mid-to-late 1860s. Although he had been an influential Mormon leader both in England and Utah, Harrison—along with Godbe—was considered an apostate and excommunicated.

Although the most exuberant of these three, the facade of the stone-clad 1889 Crane Building/Royal Café (right), designed by Kletting, was later covered with metal siding, forgotten, and recently destroyed. Remaining is the restored Karrick Block (middle), a Victorian structure and one of Kletting's first commissions in Utah. It was built for Lewis C. Karrick, a mining entrepreneur who served on the city council in the 1880s. For years, there were offices and a gambling parlor upstairs, along with eight rooms for prostitutes. Kletting also designed the restored Neoclassical Lollin Block (left), for John Lollin, a mining, hotel, restaurant, and saloon businessman from Denmark.

The three-story Keith Building (above) was built in 1902, during the third of three consecutive decades of adjoining construction after the Karrick Block in 1887 and the Lollin Block in 1894. Designed by Frederick A. Hale, the Keith Building was constructed at a cost of $150,000 to house Keith's dry goods store. David Keith and his close friend, Thomas Kearns, were the major owners of the Silver King Mine in Park City, which produced $10 million in wealth, allowing them to purchase the *Salt Lake Tribune* in 1905 and invest in numerous banks and businesses. The symmetrical facade is fairly flat but features a few classical ornaments. For over 80 years, it housed Zion's/Weller's Bookstore and its one-million-volume inventory.

Richard K.A. Kletting's front elevation drawing for the Utah Commercial and Savings Bank (left) closely resembles the actual bank facade. The 1889 date on the drawing has worn off on the building. After arriving in Utah in 1884 from Denver, Kletting quickly became one of the city's brightest architectural lights. German-born and trained in European classicism, he was a master of beautifully proportioned, symmetrically composed designs and was equally adept in a wide variety of styles. He was killed by an automobile in 1943.

Of the three excellent examples of Richardsonian Romanesque, or Romanesque Revival, in Salt Lake City, the Utah Commercial and Savings Bank is the smallest and the only one built of local red sandstone. It was constructed between 1888 and 1890 for English-born building contractor Francis Armstrong while he was serving as mayor. The facade is veneered in heavily rusticated, smooth, carved stone and dressed in a variety of shapes and textures to achieve a massive yet delicate and picturesque effect.

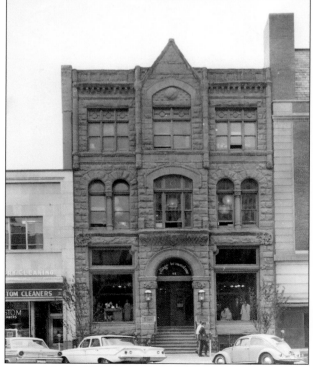

The Fritsch Block was built in 1890 to house an investment company founded by John A. Fritsch, who arrived from Germany a year earlier. The building had a variety of uses, including boarding and hotel rooms. Its longest tenant was Guthrie Bicycle, located there from the early 1930s until 2011. For decades, several well-known Utah artists have maintained studios here. The Fritsch Block is an unaltered example of the recently named Victorian Romanesque style. It was designed by Carroll and Kern, the short-lived but most productive architectural firm during the city's building boom from 1889 to 1891.

In Salt Lake City, there are three outstanding examples of the Roman-arched architectural style known as Romanesque Revival or Richardsonian Romanesque. Brooks Arcade is one of them. Only its 12-inch stone facade remains, as the rest of the building was replaced in the 1990s by a new structure. It was designed and built in 1890–1891, with Dallas and Hedges as architects. German-born Julius G. Brooks and his wife, Fanny, came to Salt Lake City as two of the city's earliest permanent Jewish residents and earned wealth through real estate and mercantile endeavors. The arcade's Roman-arched window bays and heavily-textured stone walls are features of the Romanesque Revival style, which was begun in Boston in the 1870s by the eccentric architect and namesake Henry Hobson "H.H." Richardson.

The Hooper Building was another downtown Romanesque Revival commercial structure. Long gone from the scene, it was eight bays wide and featured both smooth and rusticated stone, upper Roman-arched windows, a central bay window, and a large, round-arched entry portal. As its signage indicates, the Hooper housed a variety of stores and businesses. It was designed by Richard Kletting and supervised by German-born-and-trained A. Reif, described in an 1892 publication as "one of the leading architects in the country."

Similar to the Hooper Building was the Board of Trade Building, also five stories tall and featuring an impressive, Roman-arched entry; a facade of smooth, rusticated, and carved stone; large Roman-arched windows; and an ornamental cornice and parapet. The building housed a dry goods store on the main floor and professional offices above.

One of city's the most impressive downtown buildings was the looming Commercial Block, or Commercial National Bank, usually known as the Beason Building. Built in 1891, its rusticated stone facade and corner oriel tower were distinctive. The Victorian block featured a tall and highly ornamental cornice, with multiple bands of dentils, brackets, and crown moldings. Destroyed many decades ago, it was the first major project in Utah designed by the newly arrived Frederick A. Hale after his successful career in Denver.

The Auerbach Building was similar in height, width, and shape to the Commercial Block but with a smoother stone facade. A highly successful Jewish merchant, Auerbach intended for his big department store to compete with ZCMI, and its sign proclaimed itself "Utah's Most Popular Department Store." The structure was first known as the Knutsford Hotel and was built of granite for $750,000. The 132-foot-by-132-foot building boasted 250 guest rooms when it was built in 1891. Its architects were Mendelsohn, Fisher and Lowrie of Omaha. The oriel corner tower, four-story slanted bay windows, and fanciful parapets show its picturesque Victorian influences.

As the business ventures of the Walker brothers flourished, they built newer and larger stores to replace the small pioneer ones. The three-story Walker Brothers Mercantile block was later expanded two stories in height (below). Designed by Carroll and Kern, it is interesting to compare this building with the Dooly Block, also designed in 1891, by Chicago architect Louis Sullivan. The Walker Building is nearly all glass along the main floor and features highly ornamental carved stone in the parapets and above the top corner lintels. Both buildings feature Roman-arched windows along the upper floor, but the Dooly Block's exterior is much flatter and more restrained—more "modern," Sullivan might have said.

The Sears Roebuck & Co. Building is actually the old Walker Building with two stories of modern windows built atop the older three-story building. To enhance compatibility, the upper windows were aligned directly above the original, Roman-arched ones.

Famous as the "father of the skyscraper" and employer-mentor of Frank Lloyd Wright, Chicago-based Louis Sullivan designed the Dooly Block, his only Utah building, in 1891–1893. It is attributed to his firm, Adler and Sullivan. When compared to the other Victorian and Romanesque-influenced structures being designed by local architects, Sullivan's effort is modest in form and texture. It is far less exuberant than his own work in the East, such as the flamboyantly decorative Guaranty Building in Buffalo. Perhaps the project was subdued by financial reverses due to the Panic of 1893. The building's owner, John C. Dooly, has also planned to erect a large "Ontario Hotel" next door, but this project was never built. Despite its celebrity architect, the Dooly Block was razed in 1964.

The picturesque Victorian Romanesque facade of the 62-foot-by-119-foot Dinwoody Block likely still exists behind the present flat, blank, and windowless facade, which entirely conceals it. The polychromatic storefront, with its large Roman-arched windows alternating on three of its six floors, was designed by John Bowman and built in 1890 for the Dinwoody Furniture Company. Henry Dinwoody's store was Utah's first major pioneer furniture business, starting in 1855. The block is one of the city's few architecturally significant commercial buildings not to be either razed or restored.

The Bertolini Block, one of the few surviving commercial buildings associated with the city's ethnic minority population, was built in 1891–1892 by Ignazio Bertolini for $5,000. He was an Italian immigrant and real estate developer who housed his business and residence in the small, two-story building. Designed by architect William Carroll, it is Victorian Romanesque in style and has been restored. Various grocery stores, cafés, and ethnic businesses also occupied the block.

Its round, tripartite windows made the Grant Brothers livery one of the city's most picturesque downtown buildings. Designed by Richard K.A. Kletting, the 110-foot-by-330-foot, brick-and-stone structure was built in 1888. The company's president was Herbert J. Grant, later president of the LDS Church.

John C. Craig of Chicago and Salt Lake City designed the Herald Building, constructed in 1905. It housed the *Salt Lake Herald*, a newspaper published between 1870 and 1920, which favored Mormons and Democrats and attempted to minimize conflicts between Mormons and Gentiles. For 50 years, it was one of the city's three major newspapers. Since the paper's demise, the building has housed Utah's oldest continuously operating restaurant, Lamb's, which still occupies the main floor.

The seven-story McCornick/Crandall Block is one of the most intact of the few downtown buildings surviving from the 1890s. It was designed by Omaha architect Eric Mendelssom and built from 1891 to 1893. William S. McCornick, an 1873 immigrant from Canada, had the block erected to house his W.S. McCornick and Company Bank, once the largest between the West Coast and the Missouri River. The $300,000 block is missing its classically columned east portico, but its sandstone-clad exterior is otherwise preserved.

The Newhouse Building faced the Boston Building across Exchange Place. They were to have been matched by two similar towers anchoring the east side of the one-block-long street, but due to financial reversals, those were never built. Newhouse and his mining cohorts were successful, however, in constructing the Commercial Club, the Mining and Stock Exchange, and the Newhouse Hotel, creating a business area now know as the Exchange Place Historic District. Born in New York, the son of Russian-Jewish immigrants, Newhouse created a financial empire only to lose it and end up living in a Paris apartment, where he died in 1930.

To create a new business district, a "Western Wall Street" to compete against the Mormon district centered three blocks to the north, mining magnate Samuel Newhouse had the near-twin Boston and Newhouse Buildings constructed. A part owner in New York City's famous Flatiron Building, Newhouse called upon New York architect Henry Ives Cobb to design his two business towers, considered by some to be Utah's first skyscrapers. Built between 1908 and 1911 of modern steel-frame construction and clad with Indiana limestone, the buildings are strongly classical in their exterior expression. Like a Greek or Roman column, their 11-story heights are visually divided into three vertical parts—a two-story "base," a seven-story "shaft," and a two-story "capital."

The Neoclassical Revival Mining and Stock Exchange was erected in 1908 in what became the Exchange Place Historic District. During the uranium boom of the 1950s, it exchanged more shares of stock daily than the New York Stock Exchange in New York City. Built with a sandstone facade, it has an Ionic-columned, three-bay front, a classical entablature, and a triangular pediment. Born in 1865, Chicago-based architect John C. Craig designed the exchange, along with the nearby New Grand Hotel, the nonextant Eagle Gate Apartments and Shubrick Hotel, and the Salt Lake Herald Building.

German-born brewer Albert Fisher had this three-story commercial building erected in 1903 for $25,000. Richard K.A. Kletting, who also designed Fisher's west side mansion, was the architect. The building housed the Utah Federation of Labor and its labor unions. Initially, it also contained offices and an auditorium capable of seating 500. In 1913, Fisher remodeled the interior, converting it to the Plandome Hotel.

Richard K.A. Kletting's McIntyre Building claimed to be Utah's first modern fireproof building. It was completed in 1908–1909 with a steel-reinforced superstructure; metal windows, railings, and trim; and marble and plaster interior floors and walls—all nonflammable materials. The building is one of Utah's three examples of the Sullivanesque commercial style, celebrating vertical expression and building height rather than the traditional tripartite division of a facade. Its upward-reaching piers and foliated cartouches in the cornice and window spandrels recall Sullivan's similar use of carved stone ornamentation. This was Utah's first and tallest "skyscraper" until the Boston and Newhouse Buildings were completed two years later. The McIntyre Building was constructed for about $180,000 for William H. McIntyre Sr., who became wealthy through mining and ranching investments.

Although the terra-cotta-clad, Roman arch–topped Felt and Kearns Buildings are similar in style and were built on Main Street at about the same time, between 1909 and 1911, they were designed by different architects. Richard Kletting designed the Sullivanesque Felt Building (pictured), built at a cost of $150,000 for local businessman Orange J. Salisbury and named after a partner in his investment company. The clean-looking facade remains intact, including the medallions containing classical busts under the arches and the building's name below the dentiled cornice.

The Kearns Building is an exceptionally pure and intact example of Sullivanesque architecture. Built between 1909 and 1911, the 10-story, steel, brick, and reinforced concrete building is modern in concept and material. Like Louis Sullivan's Wainwright Building in St. Louis and the Guaranty Building in Buffalo, the Kearns Building facade emphasizes verticality with its soaring, unbroken piers separating recessed stacks of paired windows and terminating below the cornice in ornamental arches. Los Angeles architects Parkinson and Bergstrom highlighted the facade's wall surfaces with bas-relief ornamentation in terra-cotta from Gladding-McBean of Los Angeles. The building's owner, Thomas Kearns, became a multimillionaire from mining ventures in Park City and was also an owner of the *Salt Lake Tribune* and a US senator from 1901 to 1905.

The LDS Church built this Beaux-Arts landmark in 1907–1909 to house offices for its presiding bishopric. It was designed by Joseph Don Carlos Young and his son Don Carlos. The facade featured Roman- and flat-arched openings, Corinthian columns, and ornamental cornices. Although majestic, it was later razed to make way for new construction.

47 East South Temple may be the best-known address in Utah. From its completion in 1917 to the present, as the world administrative headquarters for the Church of Jesus Christ of Latter-day Saints, it has been the locus where the Church's top-level leaders make decisions influencing the lives of the faithful—and others—in Utah and worldwide. Designed by Brigham Young's son Joseph Don Carlos Young and grandson Don Carlos Young, the building is an excellent example of the Neoclassical Revival architectural style that dominated large public edifices in the early 20th century. Built of local granite at a cost of $1 million, the building has imposing facades that feature three-story-high Ionic columns. The interior is elegantly finished and furnished.

The Strevell-Patterson Hardware Company Building's main entry has a massive Roman arch, enclosing a delicately ornamental half-round window. Designed by Carl Neuhausen, it was built in 1903. The eight men in the foreground provide a good sense of the scale of this welcoming entryway.

The seven-story Judge Building was erected in 1907 for Mary Judge, the wife of Silver King mining magnate John Judge and the namesake of Judge Memorial High School. Mary's favorite architect, David C. Dart, designed this Railroad Exchange Building to house the offices of more than 20 railroad companies. Its ornate copper cornice is its most notable exterior element. In 1985, the sixth floor of the building was the site of the pipe-bombing murder of businessman Steven Christensen by Mark Hofmann, the infamous forger of "historical" documents.

When completed in 1912, the 16-story-plus Walker Bank Building was said to be the tallest building between the Missouri River and West Coast. As such, it received the rare distinction of being featured in the 1914 issue of *American Architect* magazine. It was the crown jewel of the financial empire established in the 1850s by the four Walker Brothers—Samuel, Joseph, David, and Matthew. This bank tower was designed by local architects McDonald & Cooper along with Eames and Young of St. Louis. Its exterior composition follows that of a tripart, classical column: a "base" of three articulated floors, then a "shaft" of ten identical stories, topped by a "capital" of three additional stories and a heavy, classically detailed cornice. On the roof is a two-story structure with the famous neon Walker Tower. Visible for miles, this three-story, metal-framed structure tells the weather by displaying solid or flashing blue or red lights at night. This landmark was recently renovated.

After the Walker Building was constructed one block to the south, the shorter First Security Bank was built in 1919 at a cost of $500,000. It was designed by Cannon and Fetzer. The first Mormon commercial bank in Utah, it began as Zion's Cooperative Banking Institution, with Brigham Young as president. Later, it became the Bank of Deseret—from a *Book of Mormon* word meaning "honeybee." Still well preserved, like most of the city's other tall buildings, its verticality is divided into the elements of a classical column, with its "pedestal," "shaft," and "capital."

One of the city's largest terra-cotta-clad commercial structures is the Clift Building, constructed in 1919–1920. It was designed by Chesebro and Winburn and displays Beaux-Arts and Second Renaissance Revival stylistic elements. Virtue Clift had it built in honor of her late husband, financier and mining entrepreneur Francis Clift, on the site of the former Clift Hotel.

Another design collaboration between local and out-of-state architects was that of Frederick A. Hale with George W. Kelham of San Francisco, who teamed on the $1 million Continental Bank Building. Built in 1923–1924, this concrete and steel structure is architecturally intact inside and out. Its Roman-arched, 12-bayed north facade is four times wider than its narrow, three-bay Main Street elevation. The facade of its two lower floors in the ornate Second Renaissance Revival style is in stark contrast to the nine plain stories above it. The bank was constructed for the Continental Bank and Trust Company after a 1920 merger orchestrated by James E. Cosgriff. The renovated building now houses a popular restaurant on the main floor.

The Thompson/Tribune Building was constructed in 1924 with modest Art Deco features. The Art Deco movement got its impetus from the 1925 Exposition Internationale des Arts Décoratifs et Industriels Modernes in Paris, so this might be a pre–Art Deco example. Its symmetrical brick facade has unbroken brick piers ascending its 10 stories. The main Art Deco feature of the Pope and Burton building is its tall, ornamental cornice of terra-cotta. Its first owner was multimillionaire Ezra Thompson, the president of several investment and mining companies and two-term Salt Lake City mayor. Starting in 1937, the building was the headquarters of the *Salt Lake Tribune*. Once an anti-Mormon paper, it became more moderate and objective after 1920, encouraging peaceful cooperation between the state's disparate religious, political, and economic groups.

Four

INDUSTRIAL BUILDINGS

One of the two or three oldest buildings in Utah, the Isaac Chase Mill was constructed between 1849 and 1852 and was one of the first automated, commercial flour mills in the West. It was designed by territorial millwright Frederick Kesler as the first of his more than 30 pioneer mills. He used a millwright's guidebook by Oliver Evans to design a water-powered, gear-driven mechanical system, which could be operated all day by just a miller and his assistant. Its metal turbines were among the first 40 installed in the United States. Brigham Young became Chase's partner in the stone and adobe mill in the early 1850s and then full owner in 1859, after which it was referred to as Young's "Lower Mill." It was one of eight buildings constructed in Utah's first industrial park. Abandoned as a mill in 1879 and left vacant, it was restored more than 120 years later following the research and designs of CRSA Architects. It now serves as an education center for the Tracy Aviary.

One of Utah's first food-producing buildings was the Sugar Factory, erected in 1852 in the Sugarhouse neighborhood. Designed by Salt Lake Temple architect Truman O. Angell, the factory was intended to provide refined sugar, but it could produce only molasses. The French company that sold the equipment apparently purposely left out a few of the essential pieces needed to produce sugar, so the stone and adobe factory was modified to serve other uses before being razed in the 1920s. In 1990, a replica based on Angell's plans was built as a visitor center for This is the Place Heritage Park.

Recently razed, the right-side portion of the 1902-built Utah Storage and Ice Company building featured ornamental graphite on its facade. This 1905 photograph shows the entire complex, most of which was destroyed many decades ago.

The brick Deseret Woolen Mills Company factory existed for well over 100 years until its demolition in the 1990s. It was part of an LDS Church system of factories that produced locally manufactured goods—a preference to importing more expensive goods or buying them from the Gentiles. The crenellations along its parapet are reminiscent of those along the top walls of the Salt Lake Temple, giving it a castellated, fortress-like appearance. The building was designed by William Carroll and built in 1888 for $25,000.

Another even more castellated factory was the brick complex erected for the Salt Lake Brewing Company. Despite the teetotalist Mormon populace, there were several large breweries in the city around 1900. This one's turret-finials, crenellations, and dentils are fanciful for a factory. It was built in 1890 and designed by Richard K.A. Kletting.

One of Utah's largest still-standing historic warehouses is the Salt Lake Hardware Building, seen here in 1909. The exterior of this brick box designed by William Lepper has since been painted and the interior renovated for professional offices. Unlike most of the city's warehouses, its plain facade is devoid of ornamentation. Inside, its tall ceilings and large open spaces were conveniently convertible to its new spatial arrangements and uses.

The J.G. McDonald Chocolate Company Building was erected in 1901, with its two upper stories added in 1909. Those two upper floors were later removed and then added back a second time as part of an overall renovation converting the long building into condominiums. Its stone-trimmed brick facade is Victorian Romanesque because of its third-story Roman-arched windows. The factory produced hand-dipped chocolate and boxed candy as well as chocolate drink. The architect was the Swedish-born John A. Headlund, who came to Utah in 1890.

Built in 1897–1898 and designed by architect Walter E. Ware, the Henderson Block is arguably the most stylish industrial building in the Historic Warehouse District. With its street-level wall and four Roman arches of rusticated stone, stone lintel bands, and Greek Revival cornice, it is a rare example of Victorian Romanesque warehouse architecture. Valuing its character, local architectural firm GSBS bought, renovated, and occupied the building for its offices in the late 1970s. The block was erected for Wilber S. Henderson and his wholesale grocery business. Built for $20,000, it is 74 feet by 100 feet in plan and 52 feet tall.

With its highly ornamental entry frontispiece and articulated, light-colored pilasters, the c. 1933 Central Warehouse possesses a type of decorativeness not common in its neighboring warehouses. It was built just before the Great Depression for George E. Chandler, who came to Utah in 1875. Still intact, its round-arched central transom provides visual contrast.

Architects Scott & Welch designed the N.O. Nelson Manufacturing Company Building in 1923 and it was built for about $100,000. For 35 years, it produced plumbing and heating equipment. After 1956, it was occupied by the Salt Lake Stamp Company, and for the last two decades, it has housed condominiums. The exterior features an expressed, reinforced concrete framework of posts and floors. Its sparse ornamentation consists of modernist motifs in tile at the top of its concrete posts and some oval sign panels.

The brick and concrete-trimmed Crane Company Building was designed by Ware and Treganza and built in 1910 for about $100,000. Founded in Chicago in 1855 by Richard T. Crane, the company manufactured plumbing and heating equipment and fixtures, as well as elevators, pumps, fans, and engines. The building was constructed during a building boom, and aside from the tripart division of its facades, the exterior is a vernacular commercial/warehouse expression. It was renovated in 1980 for a main floor restaurant and upper-level offices.

Recently renovated and converted into condominiums, the Decker-Patrick Company Building was designed by the firm of Headlund and Kent and built in 1914. Its white-painted trim stands in stunning contrast to its dark brick, creating a visually active facade. Its Commercial Style storefront remains intact. The building housed a wholesale business providing a variety of dry goods and men's and women's personal products.

Trolley Square occupies an entire city block in the heart of the Central City neighborhood. It consists of Mission or Spanish Colonial Revival–style trolley barns built of brick and trimmed in concrete. They were constructed between 1906 and 1910 for the Utah Light & Railroad Company. By 1918, there were 146 miles of track serviced by electric trolleys from this facility, providing the city's main public transit system until 1933. Between 1966 and 1971, Trolley Square became one of the country's largest commercial-retail historical preservation projects, led by developer Wally Wright and designed by architect Ab Christensen. It has been expanded further in the last few years.

The block-long Free Farmers Market row building was built of brick by the Ogden-based Eccles-Browning Investment Company in 1910. Its architect was also an Ogden resident—Samuel T. Whitaker, who had a diverse career as an architect, a superintendent of mills, Ogden police chief, a traveling sketch artist, a Mormon mission president, and director of the Utah State Fair Association. Initially, this long, vernacular building housed only wholesale grocery companies. About 40 years ago, led by the efforts of Steven Goldsmith, the complex became part of Artspace, a work-live development for local artists.

Five

HOTELS AND APARTMENTS

One of the city's first hotels was the 2.5-story Valley House, first built as an adobe house for eventual Mormon Church president Wilford Woodruff in 1851. It was built in two sections: the two-story, gabled house on the left and the 1873 Saltbox-style plastered portion with quoins on the right. Catering to LDS guests, no drinking was allowed in the Valley House. Remarkably, despite its pioneer origin, its small size, and its prime downtown location, it survived until 1915.

Built in 1877 as one of the first four-story buildings in Utah Territory, the Walker House was one of the city's earliest large hotels, looming above its smaller pioneer neighbors. It was built by the four Walker brothers who become successful businessmen, owning banks, dry goods stores, and other investments. The facade of the Walker House featured classical columns, Italianate lintel caps, and a bracketed cornice. The 85-foot-by-130-foot hotel was built for $13,000 and contained 110 guest rooms. It was designed by architect E.L.T. Harrison.

Although symmetrical in composition, the two-story oriel bay window is a Victorian-influenced architectural element. At the time of this photograph, the three-story Salt Lake Hotel offered rooms for 75¢ and $1. Note the tall, highly ornamental metal cornice and the raised central parapet. The building was razed to make way for the city's new post office addition in 1930.

The Templeton Building's architect, Joseph Don Carlos Young, was also president of the Central Hotel Company, which built and operated it. Then the LDS Church architect, Young had also designed the Brigham Academy in Provo, Brigham Young Agricultural College in Logan, and the spectacular Bear Lake Stake Tabernacle in Paris, Idaho. While these structures remain, the beloved 125-room Templeton Building was destroyed in 1959 in favor of a taller commercial-retail building. This architect's rendering anticipated four stories, but it was built six stories tall.

One of Salt Lake City's most picturesque hotels was the Central Hotel, better known as the Templeton Building, constructed in 1889–1890 across the street from Temple Square. Highly decorative in what is now called Victorian Eclectic styling, it was graced by slanted-bay windows, balconets, segmented and round-arched windows, and elaborate parapets and finials.

The Savoy Hotel, housed in the Culmer Block, was designed by architect Julius Hansen and erected in 1889. Trained in Berlin and Vienna, Hansen came to Utah from Copenhagen after stops in New York and Chicago. His highly ornamental storefront featured three types of window arches and classical pilaster-columns between the windows. A gabled central parapet contained the building's name and a clock

German-born brewer and real estate developer Albert Fisher built the limestone-faced Hotel Albert in 1909 for about $100,000. Its symmetrical, Second Renaissance Revival facade is still intact. Designed by Bernard O. Mecklenburg and notable for its classical detailing and bracketed cornice, the building was later known as the Hotel Shelton, the Reid Hotel, and more recently as part of Arrow Press Square. The structure now stands alone, its neighbors having been lost to fire and demolition, and its future is uncertain.

The one remaining hotel in the Exchange Place Historic District is the New Grand Hotel. The modest brick block was designed by John C. Craig and constructed in 1910. It contained 150 small, single-occupancy rooms and was built for John Daly, co-owner of the Daly-Judge Mines. Its two porte cocheres are gone, but the hotel's exterior is otherwise intact. It was renovated in 1989–1990, taking advantage of historic building tax credits and a facade easement.

During the period of "accommodation" following the end of the Mormon practice of polygamy and subsequent obtaining of statehood, the Hotel Utah was the first major project built cooperatively by the previously adversarial Mormons and non-Mormons. It was constructed in 1909–1911 at a cost of about $2 million. The architects of the terra-cotta-clad hotel were Parkinson and Bergstrom of Los Angeles, who referred to its architecture as "Modern Italian Renaissance." Built with 500 rooms, the hotel later received a major addition to the north in matching terra-cotta and is now the Joseph Smith Memorial Building, operated by the LDS Church as a visitor, reception, and meeting center.

As a result of Salt Lake City's rapid growth, several major hotels were constructed in the first decade of the 20th century. Among those still standing is the New York Hotel, built in 1906 for developer Orange J. Salisbury. Built with 75 rooms at a cost of $50,000, it is one of several surviving buildings designed by state capitol architect Richard K.A. Kletting. In the mid-1970s, historic building developer John Williams purchased and renovated the deteriorating hotel and revived it, converting it to restaurants on the main and basement levels and offices above.

In direct response to the construction of the Denver & Rio Grande and Union Pacific railroad depots, the Peery Hotel was built in 1910 by businessmen brothers David H. and Joseph S. Peery. In 1925, they leased their hotel to Harry K. Miles, who bought it in 1947 and renamed it the Miles Hotel. He also owned the more famous Showboat Hotel in Las Vegas. The Peery was designed by architects Charles B. Onderdonk and Irving Goodfellow. In plan, it is E-shaped on the upper two floors, with its light wells facing Broadway Street. With its bracketed, cantilevered cornice and inlaid tile "crosses," the facade exhibits Prairie Style influences. As originally, restaurants continue to occupy the large, open, main-floor spaces.

Originally named after its architect and owner, Bernard O. Mecklenburg, these fanciful apartments were built in 1912. Now housing condominiums, the building is considered a South Temple landmark and features a Neoclassical entry portico, corbel-supported balconies, and a tall, heavily decorated cornice. One source records that "after being interned during World War I because of his German ancestry, Meklenburg [sic] changed his apartments' name to Maryland." Block-lettered *Maryland* is inscribed in the entablature of the entry portico.

The Belvedere apartments were built by the LDS Church as an apartment hotel in 1918–1919. The U-shaped floor plan created a central light well, allowing for illumination in the 150 small interior rooms. Although the upper walls are of plain brick, the main-level facade features classically ornamental door surrounds of polychromatic terra-cotta. The Belvedere was designed by architects Miller, Woolley, and Evans and has been renovated into condominiums while retaining its public interior spaces and features.

Another early-20th-century triple-decker is the Swallow. Built around 1900, the apartment building featured three-story porches—since removed—with square posts and balustrades, Roman-arched windows along its upper level, and a deep, bracketed cornice. The central entry surround has *Swallow* inscribed in its entablature.

In the early 1900s, when so many hotels were being built, dozens of triple-decker apartment buildings were also constructed. Among the best preserved is the Ivanhoe Apartments. The building has a U-shaped plan with a central courtyard containing porticos and balconies. Two full-height slanted-bay windows grace each wing under deep, bracketed cornices.

David C. Dart designed this early Covey Apartment complex, which still functions as apartments in the historic railroad/industrial district. They appear today as they did here, with their classically columned sunporches still intact.

The no-longer-standing Prescott/Kimball Apartments were influenced by the Prairie Style, as evidenced by the square cornice and contrasting horizontal and vertical elements. The interlocking, crosshatched motifs between the upper-level windows are also Prairie-inspired.

Built as the Caithness Apartments in 1908, this is a good example of the strong Prairie Style influence felt in Salt Lake City until 1920. The building form, ornamentation, and detailing are all Prairie-inspired. Note the pergola on the roof. This is one of the city's rare examples of the use of glazed and misshaped clinker brick. This Prairie/Arts and Crafts hybrid was designed by Ware and Treganza, who were among the first architects to employ these styles.

The still-standing Premier Apartments is a Tudor Revival–style triple-decker building. The Tudor Revival style was popular in homes and apartments throughout the city between the mid-1920s and mid-1930s. The Premier has a U-shaped plan with a central courtyard and features half-timbered upper bay windows and a tall, central chimney. The name of the building appears atop each of the hipped-roof wings.

The picturesque Embassy Apartments have remained unaltered since their construction in the Avenues. The facade features light quoins, lintels, and an ornamental entry frontispiece. The crenellated central parapet, Roman-arched windows, and Spanish tile roof add Mediterranean charm to its revivalist architecture.

Businesswoman Sarah Daft put her wealth to good use when she built this residence for homeless women, which bore her name and later became a retirement home. Built around 1913, the classically influenced Daft Home is Georgian Revival in style and was the work of William H. Lepper. Daft had previously built the Daft Block (page 40)..

The major arterial street, 1300 East, is terminated on the north by the elegant Mayflower Apartment Building. It was designed in 1927 by architect Slack Winburn, whose career spanned from 1921 through 1956. Obtaining degrees in fine arts and architecture from the École des Beaux-Arts in Toulouse, France, he designed several major projects with classical styling, among them the nearby First Unitarian Church, also built in 1927. The Mayflower was built by and for the Bowers Building Company, a Salt Lake City firm that constructed more than 3,000 buildings in the West. Converted to condominiums, the Mayflower retains its Second Renaissance Revival styling on South Temple, recently rated by *Sunset* magazine as one of the 10 most beautiful streets in America.

Six

EDUCATIONAL
ARCHITECTURE

Brigham Young's Schoolhouse was built in 1860 to provide a quality education for his burgeoning family—he had 55 children with 17 of his 55 wives. An important Mormon maxim is "The glory of God is intelligence," and the pioneer Saints held school in the fort, tents, and homes until multipurpose meetinghouse/schools were built a few years later. This substantial adobe structure sat just east of Young's Beehive House and was likely designed by his brother-in-law architect Truman Angell. Greek Revival in style, its square tower and octagonal belfry made the early city landmark visible from a distance. It was destroyed by 1900.

Oquirrh Elementary School—named after a nearby mountain range—is one of the rare survivors of the Salt Lake City School Board's movement to tear down its historic schools. Before it could be destroyed, it was sold to the Harmson brothers, who renovated it and converted the landmark into a successful office building. Designed by Richard K.A. Kletting, the school was built in 1894 in the Victorian Romanesque style and has twice been renovated, once in the 1970s and again recently to house a children's service organization.

St. Anne's was built as a Catholic orphanage in 1900. The symmetrical brick-and-stone edifice was designed by Carl M. Neuhausen in the Victorian Eclectic style. Its central tower and lantern are Queen Anne–influenced, and the two flanking side gables have curvilinear parapets done in a European manner, similar to the front of Neuhausen's own house (page 117). The large school was funded in part by mining magnate and *Salt Lake Tribune* owner and benefactor Thomas Kearns.

Since its construction in 1906, Converse Hall has been the architectural centerpiece of Westminster College. It was named after its initial major donor, John Converse, who contributed $20,000 of the hall's $27,000 construction cost. Converse was president of the Baldwin Locomotive Works. The architect, Walter E. Ware, designed the building in the Jacobean Revival style popular at the time on college campuses. Its 1989 restoration included removing exterior pink paint and returning it to the original, polychromatic, stone-trimmed brick appearance.

Upon moving to its new hilltop campus, the University of Utah engaged Richard K.A. Kletting to design its initial four buildings—the Physical Science Building, dedicated in 1899; the 1900 library; the 1901 Normal Building; and the 1902 museum, all of which are now used for different purposes and known by different names. These stone and brick structures are all similar in appearance except for their differentiated entries. They are in the Second Renaissance Revival style, popularized after 1890 by such eastern architects as R.M. Hunt and McKim, Mead, and White.

Named after John Park, the first president of the University of Utah, the monumental Park Building was constructed in 1914, designed by Cannon and Fetzer along with Ramm Hansen in the Neoclassical Revival Style. It stands at the head of President's Circle and is visible from blocks away as the terminus of 200 South Street. The limestone-clad exterior is symmetrical, with long wings flanking a central portico supported by Ionic columns. Two pairs of columns also support the faux porticos at each end of the wings. When first opened, the building housed the school's library as well as administration offices. Its primary interior feature is a mural depicting some of world history's great scholars and thinkers. The "U" claims to have been founded in 1850 as the oldest university west of the Mississippi, but it did not become an institution of higher learning until the 1870s, through Park's determined efforts.

Architects Ashton & Evans won the competition to design the University of Utah's student union, finished in 1930. The formal terra-cotta exterior is Neoclassical Revival in style and features a classical portico, complete with Corinthian columns supporting an entablature and pediment. It later became the Music Building, and in 1980, it was renamed Gardner Hall after university president David P. Gardner. To accommodate a greater number of performances, a large compatible addition was made to the rear of the building, without making an adverse impact on its historic facade.

Spanish Colonial Revival buildings are relatively rare in Utah, but one of the best remaining examples is Columbus Elementary School, built from 1916 to 1918. Perhaps architect Charles S. McDonald was influenced by the complex of Spanish-styled buildings at the 1915 Panama-California Exposition in San Diego's Balboa Park, because the entry tower and plastered walls are trimmed with ornamental terra-cotta motifs like finials, Roman arches, and a tiled dome—all reminiscent of Spanish missions in Mexico. A new renovation for a county library, senior center, recreation center, and offices for nonprofit groups was completed in 1999.

The first Salt Lake High School was part of a tripart building started in 1897. The ornate facade was the first notable design by Carl M. Neuhausen, who became a prominent architect. One can see the classicism and deft handling of detail that characterized his better-known later works. The high school's stay here was short-lived and ended when three separate, much larger high schools began to be built in 1915.

The 360,000-square-foot South High School was the last of three large high schools—along with East and West—built after World War I. South was designed by the firm of Scott and Welsh and built in 1930. Described as Collegiate Gothic in style, its polychromatic exterior of warm-colored brick and terra-cotta ornamentation also suggest Art Deco influences. It served as the central city's high school for 50 years until 1980, when it was purchased and renovated to be Salt Lake Community College's central city campus.

West High School is one of two surviving high schools in the city from the World War I era. Constructed in 1915, it is a broad, four-level building containing double-loaded corridors between classrooms. It was first referred to as the Technical Training School. The exterior's high-contrasting redbrick and light terra-cotta trim is striking. The style is Collegiate Gothic, designed by Cannon, Fetzer, and Mullen. Its stepped entry frontispiece is majestic and continues to invite students through the doors of the highly regarded school.

Seven

CLUBS AND SOCIETIES

The Independent Order of Odd Fellows (IOOF) Hall was designed by architect George F. Costerisan and built from 1890 to 1892. The brick and stone hall has an unaltered facade featuring large, Roman-arched windows, stone trim carved in foliated patterns, the hall's name and date, and its key symbol—an all-seeing eye carved in stone. Due to declining membership in the 1970s, the Odd Fellows abandoned the building, and it sat vacant until 2011, when it was lifted off its foundation, turned around, and moved directly across the street, where it is being restored.

Ottinger Hall was built in 1900–1901 at the instigation of artist and fireman George Ottinger as a museum, clubhouse, and library for the volunteer firemen's association. Renovated in the 1970s, the facility remains a museum, housing fire department artifacts, books, and paintings. Its main feature is a central stepped and corbelled tower and louvered belfry.

The Alta Club, which initially banned Mormons from membership, was founded by Salt Lake City businessmen in 1883 and became the city's preeminent social club. In 1897–1898, the present clubhouse was built, and the club was expanded, in matching style, to the east in 1909–1910. Architect Frederick A. Hale designed the initial building and Charles S. McDonald, the east wing. The stone-clad club is Second Renaissance Revival in style. Roman and segmented arches, rusticated and smooth stone, a red-tiled roof, dormers, and balconies are some of its exterior features. The Alta Club has been renovated, and members continue socializing 129 years after it began.

In 1906, the clubhouse for the Forest Dale Golf Club was initially built as the first clubhouse for the Salt Lake Country Club. Designed in the Mission style by F.A. Hale, its broad, plastered gables with curvilinear parapets and small-paned bay windows and dormers are characteristic of the style, as are the Roman-arched arcades and exposed rafter tails. It was renovated by the city in the 1990s.

The 1907–1908 Commercial Club stands proudly in the center of the Exchange Place Historic District on land donated by Samuel Newhouse, the district's main promoter. With its multicolored walls of stone, brick, terra-cotta, and tile, the club is in the Second Renaissance Revival style. Built by the versatile Ware and Treganza, it features a deep, overhanging cornice; columned loggia; balconets; a two-story base of terra-cotta and tile; and Roman-arched windows on its main level. The key ornamental interior spaces have been restored.

After King Tutankhamen's tomb was discovered in 1922, a brief Egyptian Revival architectural movement occurred. Of the three rare examples in Utah, the Salt Lake Masonic Temple is the most monumental. Carl W. Scott of Scott and Welsh architects designed the building, and it was completed in 1927. Its Egyptian character is evident in the facade, which includes a pair of granite sphinxes, papyrus columns, a winged solar disk of Horus, scarab ornaments, and Egyptian moldings for trim. The ubiquitous compass-and-square motif in the frieze identifies it as a Masonic temple. Foremost among the unique interior spaces are the polygonal auditorium, the banquet hall, and four fraternal lodge rooms—Egyptian, Moorish, Gothic, and American Colonial in style. The Masons established their fraternal order early in the Utah pioneer period, especially among non-Mormons. A committee is currently working to fund and restore the temple.

The Elks Club lodge was designed by Scott and Welsh and constructed in 1922. Stretching well back into the block, it is one of the largest fraternal society buildings in the state. Its facade is mostly light terra-cotta and features round and flat-arched windows and an ornamental cornice. It now serves as an office building.

The Eagles Fraternity Hall was designed by architect Carl M. Neuhausen and built in 1916. The facade features ornamentally trimmed Roman-arched windows across the upper floor and a statue of an eagle with outstretched wings.

In 2012, the Ladies Literary Club—one of the oldest in the country—will celebrate its 100th continuous year in the clubhouse it built for its then 35-year-old organization. Winners of a competition, architects Ware and Treganza provided a modern, Prairie Style design for their artistically oriented clients. This is a pure example of the early modern style originated by Frank Lloyd Wright. The building is horizontal in expression, with gangs of casement windows and a low-pitched hip roof to give it a low, earth-hugging feeling reminiscent of Wright's Robie House in Oak Park, Illinois, designed in 1908 and built in 1909–1910. The design was a fitting reflection of the club's progressive activities. It was aggressive in pursuing several initiatives, including the state's first free public library, which was established in 1896, the year Utah become a state. To this day, club members continue to support artistic, educational, cultural, and charitable programs.

Just north of the historic campus of the University of Utah is its neighborhood of fraternity and sorority houses. One of oldest is the Sigma Chi house, designed by Carl W. Scott and built in 1914. It is English Tudor Revival in style, as evidenced by its half-timbered upper walls and gables, small-paned windows, and curved roofing instead of cornices, replicating the thatched roofs of England. It is still a frat house.

Eight

THEATERS, DEPOTS, HOSPITALS, AND MISCELLANEOUS BUILDINGS

Perhaps the most-used building in Salt Lake City's pioneer period was the Social Hall, the city's first public structure, built in 1852. Brigham Young had architect Truman O. Angell design the adobe hall, and it was proclaimed "the first playhouse west of the Missouri." The versatile facility was also the earliest dance hall, gymnasium, performing arts school, library, and home of the territorial legislature. It was so revered that an accurate replica of the Greek Revival edifice was built at This is the Place Heritage Park and a steel framework of the building's shape was erected above its actual, restored foundation, creating the Social Hall Museum.

The city's most architecturally impressive building of the pre-1869 pioneer era was the Salt Lake Theatre. Like the older Social Hall, the theater's loss in 1928 was lamented. It was designed by William H. Folsom in the Greek Revival style and built in 1861–1862 of adobe, plastered and scored to resemble cut stone. Note its fluted columns, classical frieze, lintels, and rooftop widow's walk. The theater has twice been replicated: once for the Pioneer Memorial Theater at the University of Utah and also for the Pioneer Memorial Museum (page 13).

Born, educated, and trained in England, architect Elias L.T. Harrison put his knowledge of high style architecture to good use in his design of the Salt Lake Theatre's elaborate interior. Although not grand in scale, the proscenium arch and three-tiered box seats are heavily ornamented in classical detailing, as seen in this 1880s photograph.

Looking back to the Salt Lake Theatre's main-floor seating area, this view shows its elegant, curving horseshoe—-shaped, three-tiered balconies and decoratively painted ceiling. Architect Harrison patterned it after the Theatre Royal on Drury Lane in London.

The 1882 Walker Opera House lasted only eight years; it was destroyed by fire in 1890. Its bell-cast, dormered cupola is French Second Empire– inspired, while its ornate window surrounds, quoins, Corinthian columns, and pediments and cornices are of classical derivation. This is one of several major structures erected by the Walker brothers. Designed by Obed Taylor, it was modified by E.L.T. Harrison after Taylor died.

The city's first Orpheum Theatre was built in 1905. The Beaux-Arts, or perhaps Second Renaissance Revival, playhouse was designed by classicist architect Carl M. Neuhausen. The first major vaudeville theater in the city, it was most recently the Promised Valley Playhouse. The still-standing statue of Venus in the broken-scroll pediment is the symbol of the Orpheum Theatre chain. Although restored by the LDS Church, all but the front 30 feet of the building was razed two decades later to make room for a concrete parking structure.

The fanciful, long-gone Rex Theatre was built in 1908 and later known as the Bungalow Theater and the Strand. Its wall-hung statues of knights flanking classical statues of women are distinctive, as are the tall, modernistic windows, the undulating first-level canopy, its ornate cornice, and its fantastical central finial. As the sidewall sign reveals, the Rex advertised itself as a "Junior Vaudeville" and "Motion Picture" theater.

The flamboyantly ornate and colorful Orpheum Theatre was built in from 1911 to 1913 for vaudeville performances. The terra-cotta Second Renaissance Revival–style theater was designed by San Francisco architect G. Albert Lansburgh, an award-winning graduate of the École des Beaux-Arts in Paris. It was the second Orpheum built in the city, but it is unique, with its facade displaying a profusion of Roman arches, figurines, polychromatic moldings, cartouches, cherubs, foliated ornamentation, drama masks, classical faces, and decorative light fixtures. The interior is similarly ornate: the balcony and proscenium arch are heavily trimmed with classical motifs, while the lobby is spatially grand. The Orpheum became a movie theater in the 1920s. New owner Louis Marcus increased the seating capacity to 2,260 and installed a Wurlitzer organ to accompany silent films. Its third phase came in the mid-1970s, when it was remodeled as the home of Ballet West. It remains a performing arts facility and treasured city amenity to this day.

The Tower Theater still exists in the Ninth and Ninth neighborhood as a movie house, but this facade is not visible, hidden behind a blank wall put over it in 1952. Built in 1926, the building's double-octagon-towered and light-quoined exterior resembles that of the Tower of London. It showed early talkies and today features artistic, foreign, and Sundance films. One of the towers still stands, and a restoration of the original facade is currently being considered.

The classically trained Richard K.A. Kletting was called upon to design the monumental but short-lived Salt Palace, or "temple of amusement." It was built in 1899 and destroyed by fire only a decade later. Kletting was Utah's expert in designing great domed structures, including those of Saltair Pavilion, the state capitol, and Granite Stake Tabernacle. Surrounded by an octagonal arcade with classical porticos and statuary, the palace's massive central dome was classically trimmed with swags and finials. To cause it to shine and glisten in the sun, salt crystal was mixed into the building's exterior plaster and trim.

After Utah became a state in 1896, its fairgrounds were moved 10 blocks west of downtown to a new Utah State Fair Grounds, now called the State Fairpark. The Coliseum was built there with an oval floor plan; a large, rounded, clerestory dome; and a Neoclassical entry. Built of brick and stone, the open interior space was illuminated by large, Roman-arched windows located around the perimeter wall.

Built in 1908–1909, with D.J. Patterson as architect, this depot was originally erected for the Oregon Shortline Railroad, but it soon became the Union Pacific Station. Like the Denver & Rio Grande depot built at the same time, it has a central section flanked by two identical wings. Overall, the depot measures 100 feet by 388 feet, with its central area being 100 feet by 136 feet. Its style is French Renaissance Revival, and the mansard roofs, small round dormers, and three Roman-arched windows are its defining features. The spacious waiting room contains large, painted murals depicting scenes of Utah history, including the driving of the golden spike at the 1869 connecting of the Transcontinental Railroad. The depot is now part of the Gateway complex.

The Denver & Rio Grande station was designed in 1908 by Chicago architect Henry S. Schalchs and built in 1909–1910 at a cost of about $750,000. A fine example of Beaux-Arts classicism, the depot measures 98 feet by 417 feet and is at the western terminus of Broadway Street. A tall central block with three Roman arches is flanked by identical, shorter, two-story wings, all beneath massive Italian-tiled hip roofs. Inside, the grand, 83-foot-by-144-foot waiting room is 58 feet tall. In the early 1980s, the depot was given to the State of Utah to house offices for the State History, Archives, Arts and Museum Services divisions. A recent renovation attached the depot to the new State Archives Building and created an elegant reading room.

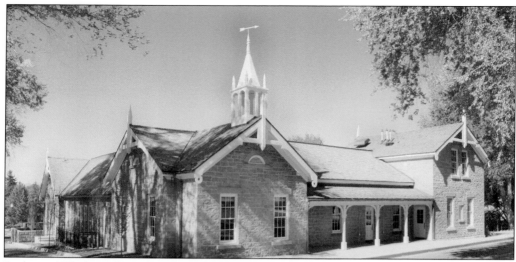

Built in 1875, the Officer's Club was constructed of red sandstone, with white wooden porches, window and gable trim, and a small bell tower. A socializing center for Fort Douglas, the club's later adverse renovations were reversed by CRSA Architects during a restoration, which created an architecturally compatible sandstone addition and returned the historic exterior and the interior rooms to their original sizes and character. Camp Douglas was founded in 1862, ostensibly to protect locals from Indians but more likely to keep watch on the Mormons. The federal fort's campus of scores of adobe, stone, and brick buildings is now a historic district. Several of its 1875-era buildings were designed by W.T. Howell, assisted by Henry Monheim.

Only two days after entering the Salt Lake Valley, a group of pioneer leaders discovered sulfur springs at the west foot of Ensign Peak just north of the city. Here, they built a bathhouse in 1850, which was followed by other larger ones later. The city built the Spanish Colonial Revival–style Wasatch Springs Plunge (pictured) in 1923–1924 following the design of Cannon and Fetzer architects. The long, reinforced concrete, terra-cotta-trimmed plaster exterior enclosed a lobby, café, recreational spaces, and two large pools, the largest of which was 50 feet by 120 feet. The natural springs were considered therapeutic, but the facility was closed in 1976 and reopened four years later as the Children's Museum of Utah. The building is presently vacant, and the city is weighing options for its renovation and reuse. The Plunge's Roman-arched arcades, curvilinear parapets, and red-tiled roof show its Spanish architectural influences.

The Territorial Exposition Building was designed by newly arrived architect Richard K.A. Kletting in the 1880s and built on the 10th Ward block. Kletting showed his skill in designing massive, clear-spanning roofs, as evidenced by this building's giant clerestory monitor. Ever the classicist, Kletting nevertheless designed what might now be called a Victorian Eclectic masterpiece. Its two towers are topped by Byzantine gazebos flanking a central entry element notable for its massive Roman-arched window.

This Victorian edifice was constructed in the early 1890s as the Women's Industrial Christian Home. It was built with $50,000 of federal funds to house 100 of the spouseless, plural wives presumed abandoned after the LDS Church's Manifesto of 1890 forbade the continuation of polygamy. The project was ill-fated, however, as its intended occupants did not want to live there. Only three women entered the facility, so it sat vacant for two years. The grandiose building was then stripped of its Victorian architecture, modernized, and converted to an entirely different use—ironically, as the Ambassador Club for men—and later razed. It is architecturally similar to the first Holy Cross Hospital (page 100), suggesting Henry Monheim designed both buildings.

The central section of the Holy Cross Hospital was designed by Henry Monheim in 1881. The south wings were designed around 1900 by German-born Catholic architects Bernard O. Mecklenburg and Carl M. Neuhausen. Its two wings are slightly different in style from the central section but are architecturally compatible. The three-story, polygonal bay windows and turreted central lantern are particularly distinctive. As the historic hospital was considered obsolete, it was razed, with the exception of its small chapel, in the rear of the central section (page 26).

Due to its square, castellated towers and overall massing, the LDS/W.H. Grove Hospital bears an architectural resemblance to the Deseret Woolen Mills and even the Salt Lake Brewing Company (page 61). It was designed by Frank M. Ulmer in 1904 and later replaced.

The Salt Lake County General Hospital was designed by John A. Headlund and built in 1911 in a late classical Victorian style. Its entry porticos, entablatures, and balustrades are typically classical, while the wings' slanted bay windows are of Victorian derivation. Originally the only public hospital in the city, it became home to the University of Utah Medical School in 1942. Like nearly all the city's other historic hospitals, it was deemed out-of-date and razed.

Mining was a major industry in Utah during the decades before and after 1900, and it produced many accidents and illnesses. The broad, tri-towered, picturesque Miners Hospital was designed by David C. Dart and built in 1903. When it was deemed outdated, it became part of Judge Memorial High School.

This 1919 photograph shows Anderson's Tower, a 54-foot tall, three-story stone cylinder punctuated by an unusual arrangement of Roman-arched openings. Built in 1884 of granite stones from the temple site, it stood on a hilltop in the Avenues neighborhood at A Street and Sixth Avenue, where it offered panoramic views of the city and Great Salt Lake Valley. It was constructed as an investment project by Robert R. Anderson, a Scottish immigrant, who hoped to earn his living charging fees to climb the winding stairs to the tower's observation deck and take in the scenic views through his telescope. His hopes were not realized, however, and the tower was abandoned before it was demolished in 1932 after being deemed a safety hazard to children.

Nine

SINGLE FAMILY RESIDENCES

Mormon Church president Brigham Young disapproved of log and wood-frame buildings on principle. His aim was to create cities of permanent masonry buildings constructed well enough to last until the Second Coming. This pioneer's log fort was a necessity, but within three weeks after the arrival of the Vanguard Party, an adobe yard was in operation for those who could afford masonry. For the others, log cabins were the most feasible option. The famous Osmyn Deuel log house is the only one to have survived from 1847, the first year of settlement. It has been moved from place to place as an object of veneration and now sits restored on the plaza south of the LDS Museum. The rustic, 15-foot-by-20-foot plank-roofed home housed renowned explorer Capt. Howard Stansbury for a time.

One of the first adobe buildings in Utah was this row house, built by polygamous church and civic leader Brigham Young for his burgeoning family. Although it was a humble building, it was later the home of mayor Daniel Wells and the birthplace of the new state's first governor, Heber M. Wells. The vernacular residence had a low-pitched roof, plain trim, and six-over-six windows.

Built in 1849 for Brigham Young on Brigham Street (now South Temple Street), the White House was one of the city's first architecturally styled buildings. It was modestly Greek Revival in its symmetry, cornice returns, and low-pitched roof, and exterior walls were of plastered adobe. It was designed by Truman O. Angell for his daughter, Mary Ann Angell, or "Mother Young," Brigham Young's second wife. It was also the early seat of both church and territorial government. It was razed, rebuilt nearby, and then razed again in 1922 to make way for the new Elks building.

Started in 1852 for Brigham Young, the Beehive House (far right) was completed in 1854. It was designed by architect Truman O. Angell, whose daughter, Mary Ann Angell, Brigham Young's second wife, lived in the house with their seven children. Brigham Young's bedroom was also in the Beehive House. In 1888, it became an official residence for church presidents. The LDS Church restored the Beehive House in 1959–1960, bringing it back to its 1888, Greek Revival–style appearance. The beehive has a special place in Mormon history and is the symbol of industriousness for the Beehive State. This mid-1850s photograph is one of the first ever taken in Utah and shows the rooftop cupola's carved beehive.

Brigham Young was sometimes referred to as the "Lion of the Lord," and he died in the Lion House (far left) in 1877. The home, with its 10 distinctive steep gables on each roof side and carved stone lion couchant above the main entry, was built from 1854 to 1856 for Young and several of his polygamous wives and children. Architect Truman Angell designed the house, and architect William Ward carved the lion. The 40-foot-by-166-foot "Big House" is made of adobe and buttressed and trimmed in the Early Gothic Revival style. In the basement dining room, two long tables were capable of seating 50 to 70 people. There were nine bedrooms on the main floor, as well as a prayer room and parlors. The second floor had bedrooms for childless wives, and the attic had 20 children's bedrooms. Brigham's grandson George Cannon Young designed the 1964–1968 restoration. It is now a house museum.

This central-passage home was typical of the city's residential architecture of the 1850s and 1860s. Unlike most other houses, the soft adobe was left unplastered. It was built for John V. Long, and Col. (later general) Patrick E. Conner, the commander of Camp Douglas, lived here in 1862 prior to the building of the fort.

The Nelson Wheeler Whipple House is one of the oldest in Utah and one of the rare few to have had its construction documented. It is also one of the best remaining examples of the Greek Revival architecture that dominated Utah for its first 25 years. The plastered adobe house was built in 1854 by Whipple, who came from New York and became a policeman, gunsmith, carpenter, shingle-maker, and journal-keeper. In the 1930s, his writings were serialized in the Mormon *Improvement Era* magazine. His well-preserved central-passage house with its wide porch, Greek Revival cornice returns, and six-over-six windows, was built for $2,000. It was restored in the 1980s for Signature Books by CRSA architects.

This home, built by fruit grower John Platt, is one of the city's oldest, most intact, and best examples of pioneer residential architecture. It is built of four kinds of material—cobblestone on the main floor and brick above, with adobe and wood-frame rear additions. The first section was built in 1856 as a central-passage home. Its symmetrical facade, small-paned windows, low ceilings, and simple trim are typical of the pioneer era. Since the 1970s, owner-architect Wally Cooper and his wife, Martha, have sensitively restored and expanded the home.

Mormons had seen a town of octagonal structures while harvesting lumber in Milton, Wisconsin, but only two were ever built in Salt Lake City. Octagons were believed by some to contain special spiritual powers. This house's owner, William S. Godbe, had been a Mormon but became involved in Spiritualism in the eastern states and became the leader of the reformist New Movement, resulting in his excommunication. Built in 1864, Godbe's Octagon was designed as apartments to house his three wives, but he never lived there (see page 109). The architect was his close associate E.L.T. Harrison.

Salt Lake City's tenth mayor, James Glendinning, had this house designed by architect John Burton and built in 1882. It is transitional and eclectic in style, owing its cornice trim and returns to the anachronistic Greek Revival style and its double cross-wing plan, quoins, slanted bay window, arched lintels, and columned porch to later Victorian and classical influences. Little is known of the English-born Burton except that in 1884 he hired newly arrived German immigrant Richard K.A. Kletting, who went on to become arguably Utah's most accomplished architect. Since 1975, this restored home has housed the Utah Division of Fine Arts.

This exuberant Early Gothic Revival house was completed in 1872 for Ann Eliza Webb, Brigham Young's famous "27th wife" and outspoken divorcée. Later known as the Empey House, it was designed by Frederick Culmer. Note the steeply pitched roof and dormers, pointed Gothic windows, octagonal chimney, quoins, and two-story bay window.

The 1862–1863 Forest Farm House, built by carpenter William Gibbs in the Early Gothic Revival style, was the headquarters for Brigham Young's experimental farm. Here, he tested various plants, animals, and processes to determine what would flourish in their new desert home. The house was so important that, rather than being destroyed, it was sawn in half and moved to This is the Place Heritage Park, where it was put back together and restored. The house has six gables and features a wraparound veranda, a steep roof, ornate trim, and little Gothic motifs in the gables.

This florid Early Gothic Revival house was built in 1879–1881 for William S. Godbe, leader of the 1860s reform effort the New Movement, which opposed Brigham Young's isolationist policies by advocating for progressive economic development. The movement's spokesman was architect Elias L.T. Harrison, who designed this house. Godbe and Harrison had been church leaders but were both excommunicated for their rebellion. The house was larger than it looks here; note how small Godbe appears sitting on the front steps. His flamboyant residence was razed in the 1950s to make room for a small apartment complex.

The Devereaux House may be the most historically and architecturally significant residence in Utah. It was the reception center where Brigham Young hosted visiting dignitaries and was also the place where the end of the Utah War was negotiated. It is an outstanding example of the French Second Empire style of architecture. William Paul Sr. designed the right section in 1867 and, with E.L.T. Harrison, the left wing in 1876 for William Jennings, a wealthy merchant. Spared from demolition and having survived a fire, the Devereaux House—named after an estate in England—was restored in the 1980s under the direction of architect Burtch Beall Jr. In 2010, CRSA architects and Paulsen Construction re-restored the exterior. Hidden ornamental details were uncovered, and the original paint colors returned the mansion to its 1876 French classicism. The LDS Church operates this historic residence as a reception center for visitors.

The elaborately detailed Gardo House was built for Brigham Young as a reception center and a home for one of his favorite wives, Amelia Folsom. Referred to as Amelia's Palace, it was designed by her father, architect William H. Folsom, and Tabernacle organ designer Joseph Ridges. Begun in 1873, the landmark was completed after Young's death in 1877. The interior featured the most elaborate moldings, finishes, and furnishings in the city. Despite protests, the revered French Second Empire–style mansion was demolished in 1921.

The 1870s brought the railroad and high style architecture to Salt Lake City. One example is this flamboyant French Second Empire mansion built for Mayor Feramorz Little. Its mansard roof, four-level square tower, dormers, ornate porches, and round-arched windows are some of the style's typical features. Designed by William Polson in 1875, the house was later razed.

A popular style introduced to Salt Lake City in the 1870s was Victorian Italianate. This example was built in 1872 for B.M. Durell of the Salt Lake National Bank and contained 20 rooms. Designed by architect T.J. Thompson, it was constructed for $20,000. Long since razed, the house featured a three-level tower with a bell-cast roof, two-story slanted-bay windows, a wraparound porch, and bracketed cornices—all characteristic of the style.

The John C. Cutler House is typical of the hundreds of Italianate homes built in the city in the 1870s and 1880s. Its two-story slanted bay window, low-pitched hip roof, bracketed cornice, ornate trim, and side porch are typical of the style. It was built in 1866 by Taylor, Romney, & Armstrong for Cutler, a woolen-mill businessman.

One of the city's best Italianate examples is the Lewis S. Hills House, built in 1884–1885. Typical of the style are its hip roof, recessed porch, and slanted bay window. Dentils, brackets, and quoins also abound. Hills was president of the Deseret National Bank, served two terms on the city council, and was involved in the People's Party, sponsored by the LDS Church. In 1928, the home was purchased by John Landa, a Spanish immigrant, to create the Hogar Hotel, a lodging house and social center for the Basque population. In 1976, it was converted to house its present occupant, Honest Jon's Hill House Antiques Gallery.

The Matthew and Angelena Walker Mansion was built in 1904 for the youngest of the four Walker brothers. Constructed at a cost of $275,000, the 18,700-square-foot Italian Renaissance Revival residence was designed by the firm of Ware and Treganza. The exterior elegance was matched inside with a Tiffany skylight and chandelier, Aeolian pipe organ, bowling alley, and wine cellar. Beginning in 1941, the mansion served as home to the Salt Lake Aviation Club. Its most recent owner, Phillip McCarthey, meticulously restored the mansion with the help of MJSA, architects.

The Woodruff Villa was built in 1891–1892 for Wilford Woodruff, fourth president of the Church of Jesus Christ of Latter-day Saints. Two years earlier, Woodruff had issued the Manifesto, which helped end the Mormon practice of polygamy. A polygamist himself, Woodruff owned several homes in which to keep his many families. His villa is one of three Woodruff residences built in a line on 500 East. The Victorian house retains its historic appearance.

From the 1880s until well after 1900, numerous varieties of picturesque Victorian styles were popular in the city. Queen Anne in inspiration and built in 1888, the W.H. Rowe house featured varied massing and roof types, a mix of materials, bay windows, and a fancy porch and trim. It was designed by Dallas and Hedges.

In 1889, local German-born architect Henry Monheim, who later teamed with the Iowa firm Proudfoot and Bird to design the City and County Building, designed the picturesque Kahn House. Its owners, Emanuel and Fanny Kahn, were prominent members of the city's early Jewish community. Emanuel and his brother, Samuel, founded the Kahn Brothers grocery store and helped create the first Jewish synagogue in Utah, B'Nai Israel. With its octagonal tower, extensive wood ornamentation, and polychromatic, highly textured materials, the Kahn House is exemplary of the city's early Queen Anne architecture. Once divided into apartments, the former residence was restored and compatibly expanded by the late architect Steven Baird.

Perhaps Utah's best example of the rare Eastlake style is the Dr. Jeremiah Beattie House, built in 1892. A variant of Victorian styling, it developed from the fanciful three-dimensional wood-turnings of English interior designer Charles Eastlake. His 1872 book *Hints on Household Taste* inspired architects to translate his lathe-turned table legs and furniture trim into architectural elements such as porch columns and bargeboards. Rather than being scroll-cut from thin boards, the extensive decorative trim on this wood-frame house is heavier and more robust than on its Victorian neighbors. Beattie built this home as an investment rental property.

The Nephi W. Clayton House continues to dominate its Avenues hillside site. Clayton was a local businessman who promoted the popular Saltair Resort on the Great Salt Lake. From 1927 on, this residence was known as the Edward A. Evans House. Its style is a Queen Anne variant called Victorian Romanesque because of its Roman-arched windows. Weathered and somewhat altered, it is a good candidate for a future restoration. Richard K.A. Kletting designed the home.

The Edwin C. Coffin House is one of the city's most playful Queen Annes. Coffin was a mining investor, investment broker, and hardware seller. His 1896 house was designed by Frederick A. Hale and features a delightful variety of shapes, textures, and colors, including an onion-domed tower, multiple gables, fancy trim, and a quarter-round porch.

One of the city's finest Shingle Style residences is the Downey House, designed, along with its carriage house, in 1893 by Frederick A. Hale. George Downey was a retired Army major who became president of the Commercial National Bank, also designed by Hale. Robust in form, varied in massing, and bold in brick, stone, and patterned shingle materials, the house was divided into apartments in 1938. In the 1970s, Clyde Harvey restored and renovated both buildings for his oil company's offices. In the last decade, energy-conscious attorneys John and Phillip Lear re-renovated the house. To heat and cool the 8,500-square-foot building, they took heat from the gray water in a sewer pipe and used a buried heat exchanger to deliver energy to the structure's 13 heat pumps. This is the only known mechanical solution of its type in the United States, as noted in a feature article in *Popular Mechanics* magazine. CRSA Architects designed the award-winning restoration.

The Beeman House, in the Avenues, may be the purest example of the Shingle Style in Utah. Designed by Ware and Cornell, it was built around 1892 for mining and railroad businessman Newell Beeman. Shingle Style was a more massively proportioned and simply trimmed response to the more delicately ornate Victorian styles in vogue at the time. Its exterior was originally dark and monochromatic. In the late 1930s, the house was divided into four apartments. Well worn, it is an excellent candidate for future restoration.

The versatile Carl M. Neuhausen designed buildings in Romanesque Revival, Second Renaissance Revival, Chateauesque, Queen Anne, and even Moorish Revival styles. For his own home, however, Neuhausen created a distinctly European-styled design possibly inspired by the architecture of his native Germany. Built in 1901, the curvilinear parapet, slanted bay windows, and porch ornaments are especially picturesque.

One of the city's most ornate and intact Victorian houses is this Kletting design built in 1890 for pioneer furniture manufacturer Henry Dinwoody. Founded in 1855, Dinwoody's Furniture benefited greatly from the building boom of 1888 to 1892, allowing its founder to use his wealth to build both this house and his large commercial structure in the same year (page 47). The house is Victorian Eclectic in spirit but also shows strong Chateauesque influences, as in its rounded tower and front bay, classical parapet window, and carved stone porch.

Before it was destroyed to make room for a high-rise apartment building, the McCornick House was one of the city's great mansions. From its hillside vantage point, its owner, businessman William S. McCornick, could look over the downtown and see his McCornick Block, one of the city's first "skyscrapers" (page 49). His home was flamboyantly Queen Anne, with its towers and turrets, dormers, and bay windows. It was designed by Dallas and Hedges and built in 1888.

Built in 1900–1901, the McCune Mansion was the first million-dollar residence erected in Utah. Architects Dallas and Hedges designed an identical but reversed copy of the John H. Matthews Mansion on Riverside Drive in New York City. Samuel C. Dallas spent a year in Europe collecting rare woods, tiles, glass, marble, and fixtures for the interior. The exterior design is Shingle Style, although its "shingles" are glazed clay tiles. Its broad stone and dark brick exterior features a massive tiered and tiled roof, turreted tower, curving veranda, and carved stone statuary. The three-story interior employed the most expensive and refined finishes of the period. There is a three-room ballroom on the top floor, with ceilings hand-painted with classical murals. The mansion has been restored and is used as a reception and events center.

The Enos Wall Mansion was designed by Richard K.A. Kletting and built in 1905 around the earlier brick Victorian residence of Abraham Smoot. The $300,000 Neoclassical/Second Renaissance Revival villa utilized a reinforced concrete framework, perhaps the earliest use of this new technology in Utah. Mayor John Sharp was another early resident, but the major expansion and face-lift to its current grandeur was completed for Enos Wall, a wealthy miner, Freemason, anti-polygamist, and president of the exclusively non-Mormon Alta Club. In 1926, the mansion became a Jewish Community Center and then, in a bit of irony, was the home of LDS Business College for the next 50 years.

The monumental David Keith Mansion was built of Sanpete limestone in 1900 following the design of Frederick A. Hale. Its symmetry, temple-like porticos, dormers, and trim are characteristic of the Beaux-Arts and Neoclassical Revival styles. Keith was a partner of Thomas Kearns in the lucrative Silver King Mine in Park City. The mansion's intact interior is among the most highly finished and refined in the city, featuring an octagonal rotunda, a Tiffany skylight, a ballroom, and elegant woodworking. The restored dwelling is currently home to a financial group.

One of Utah's greatest mansions is this Chateauesque landmark, built from 1900 to 1902 for mining magnate, *Salt Lake Tribune* co-owner and US senator Thomas Kearns. The mansion and its matching carriage house were designed by classicist architect Carl M. Neuhausen and built for $250,000—remarkably, only a quarter of the cost of the McCune Mansion. The exterior walls are of Sanpete limestone, and the corner towers, Ionic-columned porte cocheres, and French-style dormers are a few of its exceptional features. The interior, severely damaged by fire but since restored, is equally impressive, with high-end finishes of imported oak, mahogany, and red marble. Experiencing heavy weathering, the ornate exterior walls were restored from the 1970s through the 1990s. It now serves as the Utah governor's mansion.

The James D. Wood residence was one of several South Temple mansions demolished for new construction. Built of Sanpete limestone, it was a small example of the rare Chateauesque style initially inspired by King Francis I of France in the early 16th century and popularized in late-1800s America. The dwelling's forms might be considered Queen Anne, but its rounded towers, veranda, portico, domed roof, and classical detailing are Chateauesque. Carl M. Neuhausen designed the 20-room home. Woods, the owner of oil fields and one of the world's largest cattle ranches, was killed by a train in 1961.

This pristine example of Neoclassical Revival architecture was designed in 1911 by Richard K.A. Kletting for financier William W. Armstrong and his wife, Eva. The plan, which appears to be based on prototypes created in the mid-1500s by Italian architect Andrea Palladio, features a projecting main wing and two smaller flanking rear wings. The symmetrical facade is characteristically classical, with a large, three-bay portico of four Ionic columns supporting an entablature and low-pitched pediment. Armstrong, the founder and president of National Copper Bank, was elected to the Utah state senate in 1917 but chose instead to provide World War I assistance as Utah's federal food and fuel administrator. The elegant Armstrong House has been lovingly maintained.

Gill S. Peyton had this home built in 1896 but sold it to entrepreneur William S. McIntyre (see page 52) in 1901. It was designed by Walter E. Ware prior to his partnering with Alberto Treganza and shows that Ware was an outstanding designer in his own right. Extravagantly detailed, it features a tall portico with Corinthian columns, a half-round side bay and porch, classical dormers, balustrades, cornices, and a veranda.

The 1894 William Nelden House is an exceptional example of the Georgian Revival style, a favorite throughout 18th-century America. Nelden, who came from the East, had architect Frederick A. Hale prepare the design. Its symmetry, rounded central portico, broken-scroll dormers, widow's walk, Ionic columns, and classical cornices and balustrades are all typical of the style. Nelden was a founder and president of the Nelden-Judson Drug Company, an intermountain wholesaling business.

The seven historic houses on Haxton Place stand in a planned development started in 1909 by Englishman Thomas Griffin. Among his architects for the project were F.A. Hale and Bernard O. Mecklenburg. Griffin's intention was to create a copy of his same-named childhood home in London. Several prominent families lived in this exclusive urban neighborhood, which excluded residents of color. This classically appointed, two-story dwelling at 12 Haxton Place is typically Georgian Revival.

Scores of Prairie Style houses were built in Salt Lake City just after Frank Lloyd Wright created the style in Illinois around 1900. At least five architects who were working in the Chicago area at the time came back to Utah and employed the style here, often in pure forms Wright might have approved of. The overall horizontality, low-pitched hip roof, deep eaves, gangs of tripled casement windows, and brick piers supporting a wide porch roof are some of the Prairie features in the Howard McKean residence (seen here) built in 1919–1920 for $9,000 in the Federal Heights neighborhood. Its exterior and interior were recently meticulously restored by Jack Livingood, the president of Big D Construction, and his wife, Jody.

This fully developed Craftsman Bungalow was built for Owen Gray in 1908. Still standing, its broadside orientation, full-width porch, Arts and Crafts posts, beams, bargeboards, exposed rafter tails, and side bay window are all Craftsman-style design features.

Architect Walter E. Ware's own house is a stellar example of the gambrel-roofed Dutch Colonial Revival style. Homes of this style are plentiful in New England, where the style originated in the early 1700s. The choice of this style might reflect his family's colonial origins. His father, Elijah, was famous for inventing a steam-driven vehicle that was a forerunner of the automobile. His brother William was a professor of architecture at Columbia University. Ware's 1905 home retains its original visual integrity today.

This photograph of the 1918 Willard T. Cannon House reveals highly ornate brick patterns in its masonry walls and a steeply pitched slate roof. Also typical of its English Tudor Revival style are its suspended, half-timbered bay windows. The swooping roof over the entry, Tudor-arched opening over the balcony, and small-pane windows also reflect English styling. Original Tudor architecture dates from the 1500s, but this style seems never to go completely out of vogue.

The high-contrast half-timbering, steeply pitched roof, small-pane windows, and dark brick masonry with light-colored mortar make this unmistakably an English Tudor or Elizabethan Revival house. Complementing the impressive architecture is the front yard's topiary landscaping.

Ezra Taft Benson, the LDS Church president and Eisenhower administration secretary of agriculture lived in this house, built in about 1930 on Harvard Street for Leo Bird. Its round-arched windows and heavily textured, shaped-shingle roof are distinctive. The Norman Revival style was popular from World War I until the end of the Great Depression. It was based on medieval French châteaus with round towers, especially as popularized in America by architect Richard M. Hunt, who was educated at the École des Beaux-Arts in Paris and designed French-inspired mansions in New York and along the Atlantic coast.

DISCOVER THOUSANDS OF LOCAL HISTORY BOOKS FEATURING MILLIONS OF VINTAGE IMAGES

Arcadia Publishing, the leading local history publisher in the United States, is committed to making history accessible and meaningful through publishing books that celebrate and preserve the heritage of America's people and places.

Find more books like this at
www.arcadiapublishing.com

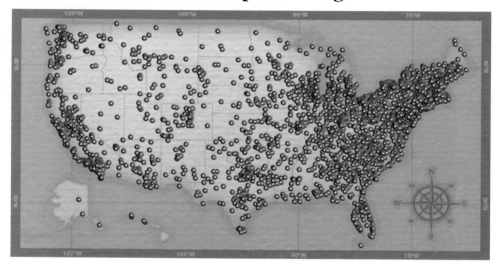

Search for your hometown history, your old stomping grounds, and even your favorite sports team.

Consistent with our mission to preserve history on a local level, this book was printed in South Carolina on American-made paper and manufactured entirely in the United States. Products carrying the accredited Forest Stewardship Council (FSC) label are printed on 100 percent FSC-certified paper.

MADE IN THE USA